Looking After a Donkey

DOROTHY MORRIS

WHITTET BOOKS

Frontispiece illustration: Cay with her own foal, Merrythought.

First published 1988
Text and photographs © 1988 by Dorothy Morris

Whittet Books Ltd, 18 Anley Road, London W14 0BY

Design by Paul Minns

British Library Cataloguing in Publication Data
Morris, Dorothy
Looking after a donkey.
1. Donkeys
I. Title
636.1'8   SF361

ISBN 0-905483-64-2
ISBN 0-905483-66-9 Pbk

Photosetting by Arjan Ltd
Printed and bound by Oxford University Press Printing House

Contents

Introduction 7

1 Choosing a Donkey 9
2 Conformation 19
3 Buying a Donkey 23
4 Settling in Your Donkey 26
5 Land 31
6 Shelter 37
7 Food 42
8 Tack 46
9 Insurance 50
10 Grooming 51
11 Exercise 54
12 Training 57
13 Carrying, Riding and Driving 65
14 Showing 73
15 Teeth 81
16 Feet 84
17 Parasites 89

18 Troubles from Ear to Tail 95
19 General Troubles 107
20 The Pros and Cons of Having a Foal 112
21 The Brood Mare 115
22 The Stallion 118
23 The Stud 120
24 Preparing for a Foal 123
25 The In-Foal Mare 124
26 The Mare is About to Foal 127
27 The Birth of a Foal 129
28 The Newborn Foal 134
29 The Growing Foal 139
30 Weaning 145
31 Hand-Rearing a Foal 146
32 The Elderly Donkey 150
33 Parting 153

Index 155

Donkeys are full of curiosity and like to know what is going on at all times. Menier, a young stallion, watches over the gate.

Introduction

Donkeys make wonderful pets: they are affectionate animals and love to be with humans. They are intelligent, too, which is the reason they have the reputation of being stubborn. Why should a donkey do something you tell him to? He will think about the situation and will consider if it would be enjoyable. But once he gets to know and trust you and becomes your friend, he will obey you to please.

Donkeys are endowed with an abundance of curiosity and like to know what you are doing and join in when possible. Your donkey would love to watch while you garden, eating weeds and rose prunings from the wheelbarrow; he would appreciate it if you took him with you when you did the local shopping and will entertain the neighbours while tied up outside the post office, enjoying the admiration he receives. He would be delighted to come into the house and show you where the biscuits are kept. A donkey can be useful, too, and fetch wood for you in a cart or sledge, carry your shopping home in panniers, keep a lively horse calm or comfort a lonely foal. One thing he will not do is mow your lawn.

A donkey is much safer with small children than a pony because his instinct when alarmed is to stand perfectly still; if a child creeps up behind him and clasps his back leg a donkey will freeze and look round to see what is touching him, but a pony will throw out his heels and run. This attitude also prevents a donkey from getting seriously injured if he catches his leg in barbed wire or gets entangled in a broken fence.

If he is not looked after properly, but is left in a field, bored and lonely, unwormed, feet untrimmed, with nothing to eat but grass, he may become a problem donkey.

It helps to look after donkeys competently if we know their history. We are inclined to have an impression that all donkeys come from Ireland, but as a matter of fact Ireland was the last part of the British Isles to introduce 'asses', as they are still referred to there. It is believed that they were brought to this country by the Romans, who used them as working animals, but they originally came from Africa and Asia. Exactly how many hundreds of years ago donkeys were first domesticated and used as pack animals and for riding is not known, but they carried the valuable bales of material on the Silk Road which ran through the territories of the wild donkeys from the Mediterranean to China, and by biblical times they were in common use.

Before they were tamed and used by man they roamed in herds (a 'pace' of asses is the correct term) through their native desert countries, and there are still wild asses today.

Knowing that they originate from these hot dry countries where they lived a communal life is a help in understanding how to keep a donkey today. They are gregarious animals and need at least one companion — if it cannot be their owner they must have an animal companion — and grass is not their natural food, nor is a soft grassy paddock their normal terrain. The wild asses range for miles across dry desert, but we keep ours in enclosed fields where they can pick up parasites dropped in their dung and reinfest themselves, and their feet grow long and turn up at the toes. Once you know what kind of life a donkey would live in his wild state it is comparatively easy to organize a suitable environment for him.

If you wish to contact either organization: the Donkey Breed Society's address is c/o the Secretary, Manor Cottage, South Thoresby, Nr Alford, Lincs; and the Donkey Sanctuary is at Sidmouth, Exeter, Devon.

1 Choosing a Donkey

Donkeys come in all sizes, colours and temperaments and in all kinds of different shapes too. A prospective donkey owner needs to decide what colour he or she would like, the size that would suit the work or life style of the donkey and a suitable temperament; it is as well to give a little attention to the conformation of the donkey also. Of course if you are going to show your donkey conformation becomes all-important, but even if a donkey is being kept as a pet there are advantages to having an animal with a reasonably good shape. When the Donkey Breed Society was formed, one of its earlier activities was to draw up a list of points which would make up the perfect donkey. This was not done so that a donkey should look as attractive as possible but because conformation affects the health and good movement of an animal. It helps to make a list; if I were buying a donkey my list would read: temperament, age, sex, size, conformation, colour.

Temperament would come first because a donkey is a pet and will be handled by you and by children and will meet other animals. No matter how exquisite is an animal's appearance, he is useless if he is not gentle, friendly and willing to oblige. Personally I like donkeys to be positively soppy. (As I can never think of a donkey as 'it' I am going to presume you own a gelding and refer to 'him' throughout the book. I hope the owners of mares and fillies will forgive me.)

Your donkey is, we hope, going to meet your friends, and will perhaps be taken to a show or the village fête. You might let a small child sit on his back, and he will need to have his feet trimmed and to meet your veterinary surgeon. You would be miserable if you were worrying all the time in case someone got hurt. We tie our donkeys beside the box when we are in the show ring, and we frequently come back to find they are being cuddled; we have even found a child trying to climb the back leg of our stallion by way of the tail while another sat underneath his tummy. Apparently donkeys are considered childproof, and thank goodness ours are, but I cannot think how nerve-racking it would be if one was not too sure.

A donkey inherits his temperament from his dam and his sire. During his life he will alter slightly according to upbringing but he will seldom, unless subject to prolonged cruelty or neglect, change his nature, so if you are going to buy a donkey it is helpful if you know who his parents are and perhaps meet and handle them.

You will, however, learn most from the donkey himself. We have sometimes gone to look at an animal and have had a small speck pointed out to us rapidly disappearing across a field. If he has just been imported from Ireland and has never been handled this is reasonable; you would understand that you had to make friends and gain his trust, but if he has been home-bred or belonged for some time to his present owners you must realize you are taking on an extra problem. You will find it rewarding to give him time and affection while you win his confidence but it will need patience and understanding on your part.

I would expect a donkey to come up to me, or at least stand still while I walked up to him. I would also expect him to allow me to handle him all over and to let me lift his feet. If he is a little shy about having his ears touched I would make allowances as donkeys are sometimes mishandled by their ears and it may take years before they are confident about having them touched by strangers; we have found this can even become a hereditary fear which is handed down by the mare to her foal.

If he kicks out do be wary. A young kicking donkey can usually be corrected, but do not take on the job if you have small children. With an older animal the iron may have entered into the poor donkey's soul. A donkey who trots up to you, pushes forward, treads on your toes and nudges you in a painful manner is probably spoilt but nothing worse. It will take a little time and firmness on your part to come to an understanding with him but he will undoubtedly become a friendly companion. I think temperament must be of first importance to everybody, but you might have various priorities second on your list. You may particularly want a very small animal, or one big enough to ride yourself, or you might have longed all your life for a black donkey, or a woolly white one, or one with stripes on his legs.

To me age is important because we have come across a number of people who have bought a donkey and found it difficult to handle, and this was frequently because they thought it would be easier to manage a young donkey. When a donkey is born it is called a donkey foal and whatever the date of its birth it becomes a donkey yearling on the next January 1st, just as racehorses do. The following January it is a two-year-old, then a three-year-old. If it is a male donkey foal it is a 'colt' and if it is a female it is a 'filly'. When it is four years old (on January 1st) it becomes either a donkey mare, an entire or a gelding, which is a male animal who has been operated on so that he cannot breed. If an entire is kept at a stud for breeding purposes he is a stallion donkey. The terms 'jack' and 'jenny' are rarely used now because they are imprecise: a jack donkey could be any male from an entire yearling colt to an elderly gelding.

The youngest you should ever buy a donkey is six months, although we consider this too soon for a foal to leave his mother; nine to twelve months would be better. Unfortunately some breeders or dealers no longer want the expense and trouble of keeping a foal and are keen to get rid of it as early as possible. If you feel you have the time and experience, taking a foal straight from his first home certainly gives you the chance to bring him up as you would want, and there is a chapter about training your donkey later in the book, but do realize he will be leaving his mother, the humans he has known all his life, the surroundings with which he is familiar and possibly his mother's milk, and he will feel frightened, insecure and lonely with new people, new food and a new home, so you will need to give him time and attention. He will require a certain amount of firmness, too, because you must start to teach him how you want him to grow up.

When a donkey is a yearling, a two-year-old or even a three-year-old, he is a *very* lively young man. This is when he must be trained, and he will be strong and perhaps wilful. If you are young and strong too it is an ideal time to have a donkey but he will need plenty of exercise and a donkey cannot be ridden or seriously driven until he is four years old, so you will have to exercise him 'in hand', (i.e. leading him) unless he has another animal of a similar age to play with.

A donkey of six or seven years is young enough to drive or ride, to show or to breed from, and the most energetic part of his training should have been accomplished for you. He will still need firm handling but he should be more circumspect and easier to manage.

I like donkeys best of all, I think, from about fourteen years onwards, when they are calm and rather slower in their movements, although they will still enjoy a good canter around their paddock when the wind is in their tail. Our twenty-plus donkeys have a great gallop round the field when in the mood. If a donkey has had a reasonable start in life and been well cared for he should live to be at least thirty years old, and although settled in his ways by then, he will make a calm, loving pet. Chapter 32 talks about elderly donkeys.

Another point to consider is whether you would like a mare or a gelding. Unless you are taking up breeding seriously and intend to run a first-class registered stud you do *not* want an entire male donkey. Running a donkey stud is a job for an expert: you are responsible for a number of other people's animals as well as your own; it entails much hard work and I promise you there is no profit in it. To own a stallion donkey as a pet is unfair to the donkey; all his thoughts throughout his life will be on mating and unless you are able to guarantee him a suitable number of mares he will be frustrated and unhappy and therefore unreliable. He might appear to be contented and docile while he is living alone with you but when he meets another male donkey or a mare he may become unmanageable. He will spend his days and nights shouting as loudly as he is able, hoping to hear a mare answer from some distant hill, and if he does discern an answering bray he will move heaven and earth, fence and hedge, to get to her, and as donkeys are intelligent they are excellent escapologists.

A donkey gelding, however, is a perfect pet; his thoughts will be divided between you and his food. Having a male donkey castrated not only prevents him desiring a mare but also removes his antagonism towards other male donkeys.

A donkey mare is, I think, sometimes more manageable and affectionate by nature, but she can be awkward when she is in season, which is the time she is able to conceive a foal and therefore accept a stallion; a mare comes into season every three weeks throughout the year. Some mares hardly indicate at all when they are in season, but a few are slightly irritable and obstinate and may shout, hoping there is a stallion within earshot.

If you think you would like to have a foal some time in the future you must of course have a mare or filly, and if you intend to breed it becomes important to make sure your donkey has good conformation as well as temperament, because you will be passing both on to the foal, and it would be wise to buy a mare who is registered in the Donkey Breed Society (D.B.S.) Stud Book. This will mean that she has either been passed by two qualified judges and a veterinary surgeon as being suitable for breeding or she has been bred from two animals who are already in the Stud Book. Then if she is covered by a Stud Book stallion the foal, if it is a filly or is gelded, will automatically qualify for inclusion in the Stud Book provided you are a member of the Donkey Breed Society. If it is a stallion, because the Donkey Breed Society are so particular about breeding stock, he will have to be examined by a vet and two inspectors before he is allowed into the Stud Book. One word of warning: if you are offered a 'registered' donkey, make quite sure he or she is actually in the Stud Book. Ask for the Stud Book number, or if there is any doubt in your mind ask to see the Donkey Breed Society Stud Book Card. If you buy the donkey the society will transfer ownership to you.

The size of your donkey depends on your preference and on what you intend to do with him. If you want to drive him it may be easier to find a trap and harness for a larger donkey; if you already have a vehicle you would need to buy a donkey to fit. Should your children want to ride, it might, again, be wiser to get a larger donkey or the children will grow out of him quickly, and it would certainly be an advantage to have an animal who was used to being ridden as it is difficult to teach donkey and child at the same time. If he is to be ridden do not forget that a donkey matures later than a horse and children must not ride him until he is four years old.

As with horses and ponies, donkeys are measured in 'hands' from the withers (the highest part of their shoulders) to the ground. A hand is 4 inches, so that a donkey described as being 9 hands high (9 hh) would measure 36 inches, whilst a 10-hand donkey (10 hh) would obviously be 40 inches. The in-between heights are measured in inches and half-inches. The Donkey Breed Society defines the height as follows: *Miniature:* Under 9 hands. *Small Standard:* 9 hands to 10 hands. *Standard:* Over 10 hands to 11 hands. *Large Standard:* Over 11 hands.

Very large donkeys are, of course, much stronger than smaller ones; they need more food and slightly higher fencing round their paddocks.

Cay, a miniature donkey when a foal.

If you would like a small pet I would recommend a small standard as miniature donkeys are valuable and command a high price. True miniatures, under 36 inches, are rare. Although there are nearly 4,000 donkeys in the Donkey Breed Society Stud Book I can find less than ten registered as miniatures. If you are thinking of buying an adult miniature donkey you must either ask for his official certificate of measurement or measure him yourself. If he is exactly 36 inches he is no more valuable than a donkey of 37, 38 or 39 inches; he must be *less* than 36 inches. If you are offered a foal remember that it is impossible to be sure that a young donkey will grow up to be a miniature even though both his parents are under

36 inches, as a well fed and cared-for foal is likely to grow a little taller than his parents. Donkeys continue to grow for at least four years and a small two-year-old will put on another inch or so.

Unless you are going to breed from or show a donkey, his conformation does not much matter provided you find him pleasant to look at, and I must admit that the donkeys I have loved best have been of a rather doubtful shape which would never get into the Stud Book, but do remember that conformation affects his health and it will save anguish and expense if the donkey you buy is fit and well. On the other hand there is nothing that can give more satisfaction than 'rescuing' a miserable, timid donkey and gradually (it takes more time than one would expect) transforming him into a happy, healthy and confident animal.

If you are thinking of taking on a donkey which you suspect might have a problem with his health you must get a veterinary surgeon to give him a thorough examination. We will hope that he is only suffering from neglect, and with good food, worming, de-lousing, perhaps some medication and tooth filing, and much tender care, he will gradually become healthy and affectionate. If, however, you get a report that he has some incurable complaint and will need constant veterinary attention and nursing I would advise you to get in touch with the Donkey Sanctuary at Sidmouth at once and tell them all about him. They have the knowledge and facilities to care for an ill donkey and will give him expert attention day and night.

Colour is easy; you can see what colour a donkey is. But remember that a black donkey becomes rather rusty in the winter when his hair is long, and a rather dull brown in winter can become a rich colour when he has moulted out in the summer. White donkeys often do not have a cross at all, as they are descended from the beautiful Egyptian or Damascus Ass, and what we call 'broken-coloured' donkeys which are either piebald (black-and-white) or skewbald (any other colour or colours and white) sometimes have no cross or only a line through their coloured patches. At one time broken-coloured donkeys were more valuable than the plain coloured animals because they were rare, but now many have been bred and there should be little difference in price, although any donkey which is a beautiful or an unusual colour — a

(Above) *A black stallion, Rutilus, in his summer coat. Breeding for colour is full of hazards: we never predicted a black foal from Barnabas, who is grey, and a pale pink dam, Angelina. (Below) Donkeys come in various colours: Esmeralda and Dandylion Handsome in front, followed by Huggy, Bridget and Sally.*

chestnut, a pink (which is a chestnut roan) or a dappled donkey for instance — must demand a slightly higher price in the open market. A roan donkey is one in which the colour is mixed evenly with white.

In the horse world a white horse is always known as a 'grey' but with donkeys white donkeys are white and grey donkeys can vary from the palest lavender grey to dark steely grey or donkey-grey. All colours look better in the summer coat. A very light-coloured donkey shows off his cross beautifully but he is more difficult to keep stain-free. Donkeys are inclined to lie down in the wrong places and get what are politely known as 'stable stains'.

Brown donkeys can vary too from a greyish donkey-brown to a striking reddish colour or a shiny dark brown. Again one can only

Nellie is white and has no cross. She has dark eyes and a grey muzzle; some white donkeys show pink flesh.

appreciate their coats in the summer, but stains do not show so much. Some donkeys have black crosses, some dark brown. Some have a very thin but pronounced cross, like our stallion Barnabas, who often passes this characteristic on to his progeny. The cross is composed of a coarser texture of hair and can sometimes be discerned even on a black donkey. Some donkeys have dark rings round their legs or marks on the sides of their throats, and these and the cross indicate how closely connected a donkey is to a zebra.

Nearly all donkeys are white or pale under the belly and sometimes the light colour creeps up their chests and down their legs. Most donkeys have a white nose, often set off by a dark muzzle, and some have light rings round their eyes. There are a few donkeys that have no white on them at all and these include the Bulgarian donkeys which have been introduced to this country by The Lady Plurenden. We are told that in former times when donkeys were often used for smuggling, being sure-footed and soft of step, a black-nosed donkey, which could not be seen in the dark, was highly esteemed.

If you intend to show your donkey conformation becomes all-important and you must get an animal who has already been winning in the show ring, or a young donkey with winning parents, unless you have a wonderful eye for conformation or a friend who is a donkey judge who will help you choose your competitor. Chapter 2 will give you more information about conformation and Chapter 14 about showing.

When the final choice is made I would not be at all surprised if your donkey actually chooses you — donkeys, like cats, can organize their own lives; you may think that what you are looking for is a small black mare but when you go to see some donkeys that are for sale you will be completely taken over by a large grey gelding who insists that you are the owner he has been looking for all his life. He will be quite right and you will never regret having changed your mind.

2 Conformation

Does it really matter at all about the shape of a donkey or what he looks like unless you are going in for showing or breeding? Some of my favourite donkeys have certainly not been those who could win any prizes in the show ring, although I have loved other, prize-winning, donkeys very much too. A donkey's character means more than his looks.

However, if you are breeding from a donkey conformation does matter, because the shape of a donkey affects his fitness, and you don't want to pass on bad conformation. The rules of conformation set out by the Donkey Breed Society for judging in the show ring are based entirely upon health and the ability of the donkey to do what work might be required of him, which in these days generally means suitability to be driven or ridden. Briefly, the points of a donkey as set out by the D.B.S. and the reasons for their desirability are as follows:

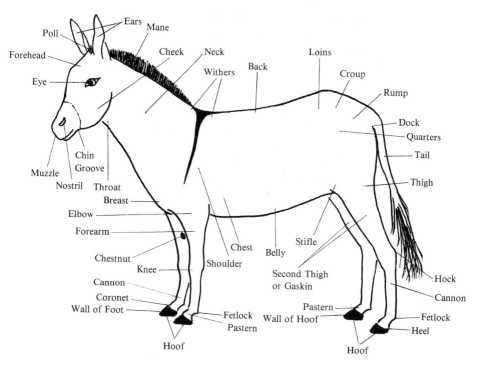

The points of a donkey.

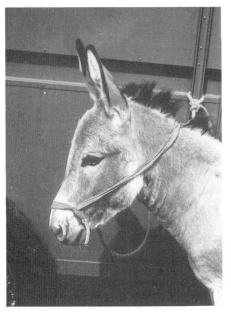

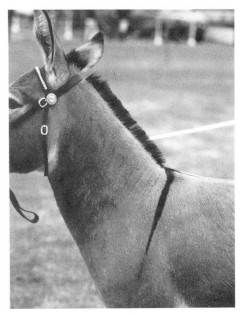

A pretty little head with dished face, ears well set and not too long, and large eyes.

A strong straight neck.

A mare with a good straight, strong back.

The **head** should be small and neat because a heavy head is tiring for an animal to carry, and will encourage him to walk with it lowered or drooping.

A large kind **eye** is self-explanatory.

Well matching **teeth** obviously mean that he can masticate, and therefore digest, his food better.

A longish, straight **neck** is more supple for driving or riding than a short one, and a good straight top line to the neck (when it is concave it is called a 'ewe neck' and is not a good thing) helps him to carry his neck better.

The **back** should be level and fairly short in a male donkey to give strength. A mare is allowed a longer back as it gives more space to carry a foal. When the back dips excessively this is known as a 'sway back'.

The **ribs** should be well sprung to give space to heart and lungs which also have more room if the **chest** is deep and wide. A wide chest prevents the front legs from being too close together, which would unbalance him, especially when he is turning a corner.

Hindquarters must be long from the hipbone to the tail, wide and well rounded, again to give strength, and to give space for the organs inside.

The **tail** should be set high (horses' tails can be set too high, which makes problems when the animal dungs, but I have never

A wide chest.

A narrow chest. This becomes ludicrous when a mare is heavy in foal.

A well placed tail.

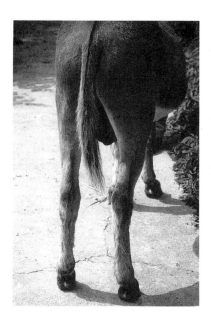

Straight hind legs. Twenty years ago nearly all donkeys had cow hocks.

heard of this with a donkey). A low tail can cause trouble when a mare is foaling.

Legs should be straight with adequate bone and a short cannon (the bone below the knee) because an animal that is being ridden or driven must have strong, well balanced legs or they could become strained with work. If he does not trot straight but 'plaits' (putting his front legs one in front of the other like Miss World) or turns his front feet out (called 'pin-toed') he may stumble. If his **back legs** curve in to the knees at the back ('cow hocks') or have a weak **upper thigh** (which is a common fault in donkeys) he will have less strength and balance.

The **feet** should be even and of a good shape; a donkey has a slightly more oval hoofprint than a horse. Obviously, badly shaped or uneven feet would cause strain and could make a donkey inclined to stumble.

A donkey should have what is known as **presence.** This has been described as a smart carriage combined with controlled enthusiasm. It is that little extra good health, good breeding and self-confidence which makes an animal a pleasure to watch.

This is all just common sense — making sure that the future race of donkeys will be healthy, strong and sure-footed.

3 Buying a Donkey

When you have decided you are ready for a donkey, and have your land fenced, your shelter built, with water laid on and hay and straw in the barn, there are two people to contact before you get your donkey. One is your veterinary surgeon. If you have other animals already you will undoubtedly be in touch with a vet, so tell him you intend to buy a donkey and ask if he is prepared to come out to your place to attend to him. Some veterinary surgeons only deal with small animals and some horse vets consider that attending a donkey is beneath their dignity. (Yes, it is true!) If he is willing to come to your new donkey ask if he would also travel to the place you buy him to give him a veterinary check should you feel this is necessary.

The other person you must find is a farrier who will cut his hooves. If you have difficulty in finding one do not get a donkey until you are successful. Chapter 16 is all about feet.

I would also recommend you to join the Donkey Breed Society; you will find they will help you in every way, and their local Area Representative will be a source of knowledge and a great support.

When we decided we would like to own a donkey, over twenty years ago, we found it impossible to buy one locally. We asked everybody we thought might be able to help: our veterinary surgeon, the RSPCA, local horse dealers, all the farmers round about — without success. Fortunately for us we found the Hon. Robin Borwick's wonderful book *People with Long Ears* and were able to trace him through it to his big stud at Maidenhead where we had a choice of buying either donkeys imported from Ireland or young ones bred by him at his stud.

The people who bought donkeys from Ruffs Orchard Donkey Stud in those days were exceptionally fortunate because Robin and his wife Paddy appeared to be willing to give endless time to find out just the kind of donkey that would suit you best, and to tolerate any fixed ideas you might have, such as wanting one with tufts of hair in his ears, or with stripey legs. We wanted a mare with short hair; pale grey so that her cross should show up well, and preferred her to have a beautiful face but cared little about her conformation, and we found our Bridget, so named by us because she came from Ireland. Bridget had a great friend who was all the things we did not want: brown, with long hair, floppy ears and a sway back — she was in foal and we did not think that a good thing either, but as Bridget loved her dearly we decided she might as well come too. We still have them both and Moira, still with long brown hair, but improved in all other respects, has always been my favourite donkey, and produced our first foal: but that is another story.

Alas, there is no place like Ruffs Orchard Donkey Stud now, but no doubt the most satisfactory way of buying a donkey is through one of the reputable donkey studs registered with the Donkey Breed Society. If you buy a young donkey you will be able to meet his sire and his dam, and probably some brothers and sisters, and he will be registered in the D.B.S. Stud Book. Breeding studs frequently have young colts for sale as they cannot keep all their progeny as stallions, and seldom have enough space for many geldings. If he has not been castrated yet they would, I expect, arrange to have it done for you before you collected him.

If you want an older donkey they may have a mare they have decided not to breed from any more, and many of the studs take in unwanted donkeys until they can be found a good home. Should they have nothing themselves they will know of all the donkey owners in their district and may well have heard of a donkey or donkeys needing a home. Sometimes you see a donkey advertised in the local paper: make an appointment and go and see him. Unless the owners are members of the D.B.S. you will need to be much more careful, and if you are not experienced with equines it would be as well to take a 'knowledgeable friend' with you. If, when you see the donkey, you think you might be interested in buying him, try to find out why they are selling. Are they moving, or have they lost their land? How long have they had him? Have they bought him on spec. to re-sell? If so, you should look at him more closely. Does he seem friendly with them even if he is shy of you? Will he allow you to handle him? To look at his teeth? To lift his front and back legs? (Perhaps a job for the K.F.) Ask the owners if they would object to a check-up from your vet. People who are genuinely selling a much loved animal due to circumstances beyond their control will be delighted you are taking so much trouble over him, and for their part may even insist on a visit to you to see if you seem suitable.

Local horse markets, too, sometimes have donkeys, although,

thank goodness, more seldom than they used to, for these are often the poor animals who have come to the end of the road and finish up as pet meat. Here you have no opportunity to have him checked by a vet, but you can handle him and see if he is fairly friendly. Remember he is penned in and might be more difficult when you get him home. If you see a donkey who seems so miserable and ill that you cannot resist buying him, and you can afford veterinary fees as well as his price (which will probably not be high unless another well-wisher is bidding against you), go ahead and buy him. Should you feel you cannot cope when you get a veterinary report on him at home, or he seems to have become malicious from bad treatment, get in touch with the Donkey Sanctuary at Sidmouth, and they will make sure the rest of his life is happy, and you will have done one donkey a very good turn.

The sanctuary will also let you have one of their donkeys, or two if you have no other companion for him, if they think you can provide a suitable home. They will send an inspector to see the facilities you can offer, and he will visit you regularly, as the donkey will always be the property of the Donkey Sanctuary. You must not feel that they are prying into your affairs; remember that they are a charity which has taken on the responsibility for the donkeys in their care and they *must* make sure that all animals are properly looked after. One of the advantages of having donkeys from the sanctuary is that they are always ready to take them back again if your circumstances should alter so that you can no longer look after them.

It is difficult to give much idea about the cost of keeping a donkey because it varies not only from one district to another and from year to year, but from one animal to another. I will suggest the approximate outlays but you will have to supply the actual figures for your district and donkey.

An average donkey will eat about 10lb. of hay per day, which is 3,650lb. or just over 1½ tons of hay a year.

He will also eat about 2½lb. of cereal each day in the summer and 3lb. in the winter, which is approximately 9cwt over a year.

You will have to worm him 4 times a year and treat him for lungworm at least once a year. Never think you can save on this by buying anthelmintics (wormers) in powder form instead of a syringe; your donkey will certainly either refuse his food altogether or will cunningly eat it all except the powder, which he will blow out of the bottom of the bowl, and your money is wasted and your donkey still wormy.

The average donkey will need his feet trimmed every two months — six times in the year — and farriers' fees vary depending partly on the distance they have to travel.

Once a year your vet will have to come and give him his anti-tetanus and anti-flu injection, and you must allow for other veterinary attention if necessary unless you take out an insurance to cover this.

If you are not a member of the Donkey Breed Society you must make sure he is covered for third-party liability.

You will also need straw or some other form of bedding for him. The amount will depend on the size of his stable and how messy he is; some donkeys always dung in the same place and need very little straw to be renewed but others mess all over the stable and need a complete change of bedding every day. A ton of straw should last one donkey for more than a year. Like hay, straw varies in price from year to year.

Land, shelter, fencing, etc., I look upon as capital outlay, as are tack, vehicle and harness, or a trailer for shows.

Looking after a donkey does not involve a great outlay each year, but there is no way we have found that you can make any money from your donkey, even if you keep a stallion and breed in a big way. Perhaps this is one of the reasons donkey owners are usually such charming people.

4   Settling in Your Donkey

The arrival of a donkey, especially if he is your first, is unbeliev-ably exciting.

When we bought Bridget and Moira from Ruffs Orchard Donkey Stud we drove back to Sussex from Maidenhead believing we had a few days to prepare for their arrival. During the evening there was a telephone call from Robin Borwick telling us that he was picking up a donkey in Sussex next day and could therefore deliver ours tomorrow at a reduced charge. As the cost of transporting the donkeys from Berkshire to Sussex was rather more than that of buying them, we naturally agreed and I spent all night, too excited to sleep, reading *People with Long Ears* over and over again.

It was February, and the next day it poured solidly with driving rain while my husband converted part of our barn into donkey sleeping quarters and we rushed round the local farmers begging bales of hay and straw. All went well except that I noticed at lunch that the meal I had cooked for poor Mr Borwick was saltless.

You will be properly prepared for your donkey and we hope he will be delivered to you on a nice sunny day. He will arrive in a horsebox or trailer. If he comes from a stud he will probably be used to travelling and will walk out of his box full of curiosity to see where he is. However, if he has not travelled much before he might have found his journey rather frightening.

We hope he will have travelled in a headcollar, or perhaps a halter with the rope tied back over his head, but make sure before the ramp is let down that he is wearing something to lead him by. If there is a side door, go in, or ask the driver to go in, to be with him while the ramp is lowered, and let him stand at the top of the ramp and have a good look at his new world. Then gently try to coax him down the ramp, leading him from his near side (your right side and his left) with your hand holding him very close to his head — even touching it — to give you the best control possible. He will probably move hesitantly at first and then leap the last few feet — so be prepared.

Again, let him look around to get his bearings and then lead him gently to his stable. If he has been trained to be led you will have no trouble, but if he is untrained this might take some time. Speak to him reassuringly with a quiet voice and if possible get him to walk straight into his stable, go in with him, and close the bottom half of the door. Continue to talk to him and show him his haynet and his water bucket; this is one of the few occasions when I think you should give him a tit-bit.

If it is possible, leave the bottom of his door closed while he settles down and gets over the ordeal of travelling, but if it is impossible to get him into his stable, or if he seems very frightened once he is inside, and hurls himself at the door, leave him in his paddock for a couple of hours, making sure the gate is firmly closed and the fencing secure.

Normally there is no need to leave a headcollar on a donkey — he will always come to you when called, and it can rub his face or get caught on a post or branch; but it is as well to keep a carefully fitted headcollar on a new donkey during the day until you are sure you are able to catch him, taking it off at night and smoothing his face.

With a trained donkey of course you will have no trouble; he will go happily into his stable and settle down — probably he will be nibbling his hay before you have gone out and shut the door.

You will also have less anxiety if you have two donkeys. While they are together they will be fairly calm; one will lead — you will soon discover which one — and the other will follow, and they will be content if they are shut in together.

When a donkey goes to a new home he is unlikely to lie down in the paddock until he feels safe and happy. Kelly and Cookie.

Should you find you have a nervous donkey I would suggest he only meets his family on the first day and friends visit him later in the week. Remember he will be confused in a new place with strange people and he needs to get to know and trust you before he makes new acquaintances.

Whatever the time of day he arrives I would give him a small feed of ponynuts (or whatever cereal you have decided to feed) after he has been with you for a couple of hours. If it is the evening, keep him in his stable until next morning, but if he arrives before lunch he will like to have a look at his paddock once he has settled down. He will probably walk — or trot if he is a lively boy — right round the perimeter, snatching a particularly succulent snack from time to time. When he gets back to you stroke him and talk to him. Always approach him, to hold or pet him, with your hand under his chin; never pat him on the forehead, as your hand appears enormous in front of his eyes and he is likely to be frightened. Later he will get confidence in you and you can approach him in any way you like.

If you are feeding him once or twice a day and shutting him in his stable at night the time you decide to do this does not matter provided it is the same every day. Donkeys are creatures of habit and, although there can always be an exception when it is unavoidable, he will appreciate regular meals.

When he arrives you may find you have got a very timid donkey; if so, you will need to make allowances and show patience. If he is frightened when you approach him, stand still near him, perhaps with a bowl containing a few cut-up carrots, and see if you can persuade him to come to you. He might talk to you over the gate before you go into the field. It is easier if you have another donkey, who is confident in you, to be with him. He will soon see he is missing something good, and it is often possible to talk to one donkey across the back of another. Always approach him slowly and above all try to avoid having to chase him round the paddock to corner and catch him. Usually it takes about a week for a timid donkey to get friendly with you, but sometimes it can take longer. This is the one time I approve of tit-bits, but they are better given out of a bowl than from your hand.

Unless you have made friends with him immediately, do not groom him the first night he arrives no matter how much he looks as if he needs it. Once he has settled in he will enjoy being brushed. Next day, unless he has come from a good home or a reputable stud, you may be having him checked by your veterinary surgeon; he will probably ask for a little fresh dung to test for intestinal and lungworms.

A very thin donkey is unlikely only to have been underfed; he is sure to be wormy as well. Your vet will advise you about his first treatment for worms. Do not attempt to fatten him up quickly with large amounts of food; he is not used to it and he will only get colic. If he grazes during the day, and has as much hay as he wants at night, it is better only to give him the usual amount of hard food. He will gradually, very slowly, gain condition; first you will notice the hollows in front of his hips disappearing and he will start to hold his head up and his new coat will come through shiny.

Overweight donkeys are more at risk than thin ones, but once again please do not immediately put a fat donkey on a starvation diet as this could actually kill him! If an obese donkey loses weight too fast it can suffer from a state known as hyperlipaemia because the fat it has stored disintegrates and is carried into the blood system, which can get clogged by the fatty particles and cause death. So just feed him normally and give him no tit-bits and he will probably be having much less food than he is used to anyway. Then gradually reduce the amount of hay you give him at night and substitute good straw instead; as much as he wants. Hopefully the fat will disappear slowly from his neck and the rolling bulges from his sides, but it may take a number of years to get him back to normal weight so do not become disheartened. The first sign will be that the crest on his neck, although still the same size, is getting softer.

Once your donkey has settled down and you are used to each other you can start any training needed and take him for a little walk around your land to explore his new home. It is better not to take him out onto the road until you are sure you can handle him and he is not going to panic at lorries or tractors. Introduce him to traffic over a fence or from your gateway to see how he reacts; try leading him past your car in the drive. Even when you buy a trained riding donkey it is safer to let the children have their first rides away from the road.

The arrival of a new donkey enlivens the whole family: you have such a lot to learn about each other. One day you will realize you really know him, and you can hardly believe that the timid little animal you were trying to make your friend is now doing his best to bully you.

5 *Land*

The first thing people think about when they hope to own a donkey is land, yet thousands of donkeys were kept in the British Isles during the last couple of hundred years by owners who lived in London, Dublin, Liverpool and all the other great cities. These donkeys lived with their families, often housed with the coal, and conveyed their owners to Covent Garden and other markets every day. They were working animals and had plenty of exercise. The families depended on them for their livelihood and they were looked after as well as possible, depending on the humanity and circumstances of their owners. However, I think, for the donkey's sake, we should be thankful for the invention of the internal combustion engine. There are still working donkeys in England, and certainly in Ireland, but they are usually based in the country and have access to a field when they have finished their labour.

If you are going to keep a donkey as a pet or for riding, showing or other leisure activity, you will need at least half an acre of land per donkey to give him exercise and a certain amount of food. This land does not need to be level or free from weeds other than those that might harm him, and certainly does not need to be lush or fertile. It must be adequately fenced, have shelter for day and night and have a supply of water.

Your donkey will be grateful if it is near to your house. He will want to see you as often as he can and be with you whenever possible; it will help you to keep an eye on him if you can actually see him from the house. If his field is a short distance away, he must be visited at least twice a day to check that he has food and water and has not got into any difficulty. Although donkeys are usually clever enough not to panic he might get into serious trouble if he caught his foot in the fence. I knew of a donkey who rolled near the gate and caught his leg between the bars, holding him on his back. By the time he was discovered he had died.

No matter how small his field, it will benefit from being fenced into two sections; if it is big enough, three paddocks are even better. Your donkey can then inhabit one paddock while the remainder of the land is being rested; this helps to prevent the build-up of parasites on the field (see Chapter 17).

Donkeys do not graze, they browse, and consequently they eat their paddocks unevenly; they usually prefer the grass in one section of the land and keep this almost bald while ignoring the less tasty areas. Most donkeys, too, only stale (urinate) and dung (defecate) in one place in their field and never graze there so the grass becomes so rank and sour it has to be kept cut. This is why I have

There is no need to clear the weeds from a field, but you must make certain there are no poisonous plants.

said that the one thing a donkey will not do is mow your lawn. The quality of the grass does not matter; donkeys like a variety of grasses and rye (which is what most farmers re-seed their meadows with) is certainly not one of their favourites. When we remember that the donkey is a desert animal we realize that any kind of grass is far from his natural diet and he will appreciate a good scattering of herbs amongst it; but you must make certain, of course, that no poisonous plants are within reach. These are the most common:

Yew is much the most dangerous plant because donkeys, who are usually clever about avoiding food which is bad for them, will eat it; all parts of the yew are poisonous and it can kill them even when it has dried. So make sure there is no yew tree near from which twigs can blow into the field.

Laburnum seeds are poisonous, so avoid having a tree overhanging the paddock; **Lupin** seeds are toxic in the same way. **Rhododendrons** should not be eaten nor should **Deadly Nightshade** or any of the **Bryonies**. Any member of the **Euphorbia** family (the **Spurges**) will burn his mouth. However, he is unlikely to eat any of these plants if he has plenty of good grazing and adequate dry food.

He is unlikely to eat growing **Ragwort** but is more likely to eat it dried in hay. As it is a shallow-rooting plant, and easy to pull out, there is no excuse for ragwort in the paddock.

I have known a donkey suffer from a surfeit of **acorns** and too many **fallen apples** can cause colic. **Foxgloves** are said to be toxic.

If you allow your donkey into the garden he will find far more poisonous plants: all the **Daphnes** are toxic and **Monkshood (Aconitum)** is very poisonous. The tops of **potato plants** and all that family **(Solanacea)**, which includes **tomatoes** and **tobacco** and the various **nightshades**, is toxic.

As well as mowing parts of his paddock you will need to deal with docks and buttercups; surprisingly, donkeys are not fond of clover, which is just as well as it is much too rich for them (but don't get rid of it, it's good for the grass). They do not live up to their reputation for eating thistles, usually waiting to nip off the flowers which taste of honey, which does, at least, keep them from seeding. They will eat thistles, and nettles as well, if they are cut and left to dry in the paddock; nettles are full of goodness and can be dried and used as a winter supplement. One plant they love to eat is bramble so do not clear it from the field before introducing your donkey. He will keep it free, too, from Queen Anne's Lace and Hogweed and I fear will demolish the wild roses, but our last fields were full of orchids, mallow, vetches, primroses, bluebells and other wild flowers which our donkeys were happy to conserve.

Your paddocks must be adequately fenced to keep your donkeys in and sometimes to keep unwanted visitors out. We would all like to have beautiful post-and-rail fencing round our land, but if you are unable to afford it you can comfort yourself with the knowledge that it needs a little modification to be perfect for donkeys. The bottom rail should not be more than eighteen inches from the ground (less if you contemplate having a foal) or you will find smaller donkeys quite capable of lying down on one side and getting up on the other — intelligence again. Your donkey will

A fence just inside a hedge will enable your donkey to keep the hedge trimmed for you without allowing him to eat his way through.

always think the grass better on the other side of the fence and will put his head between the top and the middle rail, leaning his whole weight as he reaches for a particularly succulent morsel; then he will scratch his back on the top rail, pushing it upwards; so you need strong rails, and stakes which are comparatively close together. The easiest solution is to stretch pig or sheep netting along the fence, stapled on to the posts, and kept about six inches from the ground and lapping the top rail if you want to prevent him from nibbling it.

Once you have decided to have sheep or pig netting you will find it is not necessary to have post-and-rail fence at all. Probably the most practical fencing is wooden stakes with a wooden top rail and the wire stretched between the posts and overlapping the rail, but a strong wire at the top is adequate provided you can keep it reasonably taut.

For an external boundary, with a public road beyond, you should have barbed wire on top of the fence. Donkeys are sensible and will not hurt themselves on it and it is essential that they cannot escape onto a road. It will also deter passers-by from feeding or teasing the donkey which can be a serious problem as sandwiches or pastry containing meat are poisonous, and giving frequent tit-bits encourages a donkey to nip, which provokes the recipient to retaliate. It is much better if a donkey can be kept away from the public except under supervision, even if it means having a double fence.

Hedges, no matter how thick, are useless; a donkey will eat his way through any hedge. However if you fence just inside the hedge your donkey will enjoy keeping it trimmed for you without breaking through and he will appreciate the shade and shelter from the wind. Donkeys can eat any hedging — hawthorn, holly, even blackthorn — without hurting their mouths. Privet and laurel are supposed to be toxic but our donkeys have eaten both. I think they are sensible enough to take their herbs in small doses when they have plenty of other food.

The Donkey Sanctuary uses electric fences for strip grazing and has had no problems, and I know some studs use them, but only for certain donkeys. If a donkey is keen enough to get across an electric fence he will barge it and take the consequences, so they should only be used for barriers within fields.

It is possible to tether a donkey but he must always be supervised. A tether consists of a low post or ring in the ground, or sometimes a metal stake with a loop on top to which a rope is attached which ties or clips to a collar round the donkey's neck or to a headcollar. Never attach it to a halter unless the halter is knotted in such a way that it cannot be pulled tight. A thin rope is dangerous; the thicker it is the less likely to catch round his fetlock and a chain is best of all. Never tether a young or lively donkey who may run about and be pulled up sharply causing injury. Do not tie two donkeys so that their ropes can entwine. If you attach him to a taller post or a tree he will certainly walk round and round until he has wound himself up and you may have to show him how to unwind himself. Should you tie him to a fence or gatepost you

Barnabas is old enough now to behave sensibly when tethered, but he is never left unsupervised.

will be amazed at his strength as bars break and posts pop out of the ground. If the rope winds round his leg he might struggle and hurt himself; if it winds round his neck he could strangle himself, and he can do so in a few minutes. Consequently when he is tethered you must be able to see him all the time — it is not safe to slip away to make a cup of tea or answer the telephone.

He will need a constant supply of water in his paddock, so you will need a container of some kind large enough to hold a day's supply of water but convenient to keep clean. Any kind of galvanized or strong plastic tank or bath will do, but it should be heavy enough not to tip over or blow away when it is empty unless it can be safely secured. It must be kept clean; ideally it should have the water changed every day. Never use a detergent or disinfectant to wash it out unless you know it has been polluted in some way, and then rinse it thoroughly several times. One of the jobs I really dislike is carrying buckets of water which always spill down my wellingtons, and I think having an extension to the garden hose which reaches your donkey's trough is one of the most worthwhile expenditures.

6 Shelter

A donkey needs shelter both night and day to protect him from cold and wet and, in summer, from flies. He can either have one shed in his field, which he uses by day and night, or he can have a stable, perhaps nearer to your house, for the night, and a shelter in his paddock. This is probably the most satisfactory as it gives you a chance to clean his stable, re-straw, put in a full haynet and change the water at your convenience during the day, and it is ready for him to be led into at night. If you only have one shelter you seem to be constantly picking up small quantities of dung and topping up the water. However one very simple shelter is perfectly adequate, and with ingenuity and a small 'yard' it can be made to serve two or even three paddocks.

For one donkey the shelter or stable should not be less than eight feet square — ten feet square if you have two donkeys — and it must be high enough for you to stand upright in most of it or you will have a miserable time keeping it clean. It does not matter what it is made from: an old brick or stone building has good insulation, or you can convert a part of a barn, but wood or corrugated iron is adequate. A slightly sloping concrete floor is easy to keep hygienic, but most donkeys actually prefer the natural floor — I expect it is warmer and softer. A wooden floor is unsuitable as it will rot and your donkey might get his foot caught in it.

It must have plenty of ventilation, yet be draught-free at donkey

Argentia looks out of her stable, which is quite big enough for two donkeys or a mare and foal. Note the ring on the left convenient for a haynet or for tying up a donkey. The shed is paved outside which prevents the entrance from getting muddy.

level. This is why a half door, or stable door, which is a door made in two sections, the bottom part being about three feet high, is suitable. It is best to have a door fitted to the top section also so that it can be closed against driving rain or snow. The doorway should face away from the prevailing wind, and if possible the shed should be sheltered from the hot sunshine by a tall hedge or tree. The shed needs to be dark to discourage flies so it is better without a window, but further ventilation at roof level is an asset.

Letting your donkey come and go as he pleases has advantages and snags; certainly it is less trouble for you, but we have found it more satisfactory to shut him in at night. One reason is that he will get regular handling, and therefore training, every night and morning. Another is that he will not be able to stroll outside onto grass which is wet by rain or dew, and his feet will have some hours to dry off completely, which will make him less susceptible to foot troubles. The last reason is that you can sleep peacefully, knowing where he is, and that he is safe even if the thunder crashes and the rain deluges.

The shed or stable will need some form of bedding. We like straw best and so will your donkey because he will eat it sometimes in preference to hay. Wheat straw is best, if you can get it; oat straw is acceptable, but not so absorbent. We used to be warned against barley straw because of the rough awns, which could stick in an animal's throat if eaten, but I understand that threshing is so much more efficient now that it is safe to use.

Some people like to use peat, which is useful in your garden when you have finished with it in the stable, and sawdust is a possible bedding, but it is safer not to use wood shavings as your donkey will be sure to nibble at them and you cannot be sure they have not been treated with some preservative or other chemical.

Whatever you use, give him a good deep bedding, especially if you have a concrete floor, and clean out the wet and dirty places every day, covering with clean material. If you are lucky he will use the same corner every night and save you a great deal of work; most male donkeys do this, but mares are inclined to be less houseproud.

Another method of keeping your shelter or stable clean is deep litter; this works on the same principle as a compost heap — and like a compost heap it can be excellent if managed properly and rather nasty if it should go wrong. The idea is that you keep putting fresh straw down on top of the old dung- and urine-impregnated bedding and the heat fostered by this kills any smell or germs. It sounds easy, and when done well it makes a delightfully soft, warm and odourless bed. If expertise fails it can be damp, smelly and unhygienic. Gradually the floor level rises and eventually, usually once a year in the spring, the whole bedding is taken away, the floor is washed down with disinfectant, and you start all over again. Clearing the stable is a tremendous task and needs a strong man or a mechanical yard cleaner. I would not suggest trying this method unless you have an expert to supervise, but we have found that a compromise can work well, which is to remove any wet straw and visible dung each day and then add more straw on top. This still needs a general clean in the spring, but it is less likely to become damp and malodorous.

Your donkey will need fresh water in his stable; a bucketful will be enough for the night and it can stand on the floor in a corner (turn the handle towards the wall so that he does not get his foot caught up in it) or, better still, hang it at a convenient height for drinking so that it cannot get spilt. Donkeys are fussy about their water and prefer to have it changed daily rather than topped up.

He should have fresh hay every night and can be fed from a hayrack, a manger or haynet. If you just put the hay onto the floor he will walk about on it and dung on it and most of it will be wasted. When you use a haynet remember it will stretch much lower when it is empty so hang it high enough to prevent him getting his foot caught in it when he has finished eating.

The only other equipment he will need in his stable and shelter is a salt lick screwed to, or hung on, the wall at a convenient height for licking. Donkeys need salt and it helps to discourage intestinal worms. Some licks have minerals as well as salt, and these are good, but make absolutely sure the lick you get is intended for horses and donkeys; never use a cattle lick.

It is most satisfactory to see your donkey happy and comfortable in a safe shelter and know all his needs are being supplied.

Nellie enjoying the snow. Donkeys like to go out into the snow for a short time, but they soon get cold and need their shelter.

7 Food

It is important to remember the origins of donkeys when thinking about their food. Animals that come from a desert country are not going to thrive on wet grass — and grass is frequently at least damp. Moreover grass has little nourishment except when it is newly growing in the spring, and to get enough food to keep him going a donkey needs a vast amount, which blows out his stomach and eventually makes his back sag. In his native land he would be eating dried grass, small bushes and other scrub, and all his food would be dry.

To try and simulate these conditions we need to give him dry food all year round, and the easiest to obtain are hay and straw. All year he should have a net of hay at night unless he is putting on too much weight when he should be given straw ad lib instead. The amount of hay each animal eats during the night varies: he should have just enough so that it is nearly finished in the morning. If it is all gone he needs a little more, and if he leaves much in his net or pulls it out and drops it around the floor you are being over-generous. You will need to experiment to see how much he should have, starting with about 10lb. and adding or taking away until you have got it right.

He will probably eat quite a bit of his bedding too, and if you think he is eating dirty straw you can put a wedge of clean straw under his net for him to sort through and then use what is left for part of his bedding next day.

Much the cheapest way to buy hay is to get it straight from the field when it is harvested. If you have transport and strength you can usually arrange to collect the hay and straw from the field, otherwise you must pay a delivery fee.

Your store will need to be waterproof and airy. Even so the bottom bales can get slightly damp or dusty and it is an investment to have a permanent layer of bales of straw under your hay.

There is no need to have the best hay, suitable for racehorses. In fact a donkey prefers meadow hay with weeds and herbs in it and this has the advantage of showing that it has not been over-sprayed with weed-killers, and probably has not had too much nitrogen either. It may have thistles in it, which your donkey will enjoy, but you will not, and you will need to wear gloves to fill his haynet;

Filling haynets is an arduous job. This haynet filler was designed and made by Bill Care of Castlecrete Donkey Stud.

you must always check hay carefully for dried ragwort, buttercup, or other poisonous weeds. It *must* be sweet and fresh. Black or mouldy hay with an unpleasant smell is dangerous. Make the farmer open a bale for you (a bale of *your* choice) to make sure it is dry and sweet before you buy it.

Straw, like hay, must be free from toxic weeds, and clean and dry or it can cause all kinds of respiratory problems.

A healthy adult donkey needs only hay or straw as an extra during the best months for new grass, but all donkeys need a feed of cereal during the late summer, autumn and winter months, and we find ours are healthier, and slimmer too, if they have a regular feed of ponynuts or some other 'hard' food (meaning a concentrated food like cereal, nuts, etc.) all year round. If you have a mare in foal, a young growing donkey or a working donkey you will have to feed cereal all year.

Ponynuts are the most convenient form of food. They are balanced for feeding equines and have minerals and vitamins added. An adult donkey about 10 hands high would need 2½ lb. per day when the grazing was good and an extra half lb. if the grass was poor or in short supply. This can be given in one meal, or better still divided between an evening and a morning feed. If we were only feeding once a day it would certainly be in the morning before the donkey went out, hoping to discourage him from eating too much grass while it was still wet with dew.

We make up a mixture of one part rolled oats and one part flaked maize to two parts broad bran and add a vitamin and mineral supplement. If you feed this you will find the oats make him lively and should be cut down if he gets too boisterous, the maize will keep him warm in winter and fatten him in summer, so again you can vary the mixture you give him. The bran is nutritious and helps him to digest the other food. However this means having three bags of food and it can go stale, so if you only have one or two donkeys ponynuts are more convenient.

Some people feed sugar beet pulp to their donkeys, but this must be thoroughly soaked in water for 24 hours before it is fed because it swells when wet; consequently we are back to feeding damp food, and it has little food value as it contains almost no protein and very little starch; all it does is fill the donkey's stomach without giving him much nourishment.

Cut-up carrots are a treat, and good for him. We are told they must be cut lengthways in case the donkey swallows one whole and the wedge shape sticks in his throat. I cannot believe a donkey would be so foolish as not to chew them properly but it is always better to be on the safe side. We find that most of our donkeys enjoy the green leaves of the carrots more than the roots. Eating apples are appreciated too, but cooking apples can cause colic.

There are various vitamin and mineral supplements which can be added to their feed. Everybody has a favourite and I suggest you speak to your vet about supplements — he will probably have strong views about them too. You can use any supplement for horses and ponies and a donkey would need about half the amount suggested for a pony. There is no doubt that the addition of vitamins and minerals can make a donkey glow with health.

Perhaps when talking about feeding it is a good time to mention tit-bits. I generally say these must never be given to a donkey, but we make an exception, and my husband always visits all the donkeys in their stables last thing at night before he goes to bed and gives each animal a piece of toast. He can tell by the way the donkey comes forward and takes it whether he is well and happy, and at the same time he checks how fast the haynet is being eaten and makes sure the water does not need topping up. Apart from this, extras given by hand are not allowed, not only because it is a sure way of making a donkey fat, but because it often makes them naughty and nippy. A donkey should be pleased to see you for your own sake and to enjoy a little attention and ear-rubbing, and should not need bribes. Nobody wants a pet who nips their buttons and tears their pockets, but this can happen if he is expecting a peppermint every time he sees you.

His food must be kept dry and safe from mice and rats which carry infection. Large sized metal or plastic dustbins will take a bag of food comfortably. Keep his feeding bowl clean too — dried food sticking round the sides attracts flies and rats. We always feed out of plastic washing-up bowls because donkeys dislike putting their heads into buckets that cover their eyes; their heads are shorter than a horse's head.

Lastly, keep a check on your donkey's teeth as there is no point in giving food which is not being chewed and digested properly (see Chapter 15).

8 Tack

The amount of tack you will need for your donkey will depend on what you are going to do with him, but one essential for every animal is a halter so that he can be led about and if necessary tied up.

A **halter** always used to be made out of webbing and rope but now it is often made of nylon. The flat webbing, or flat nylon, goes over his head and across his nose and the rope goes through a loop in the webbing (or nylon) at either side of his nose, which allows you to adjust the rope under his chin to make the halter larger or tighter. The principle is simple but putting it on swiftly and neatly needs practice. Never stand in front of him and push it towards his face; the correct way to put on a halter is to stand on his near (left) side facing the same way as the donkey with the rope quite loose through the two loops. Putting your right arm over his neck, place the rope under his chin with the noseband over his nose having the long end of the rope coming towards you. Then slide the long piece of webbing (or nylon) back over his ears and tighten the rope towards you.

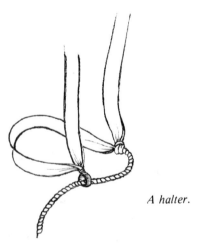

A halter.

If the halter fits properly the webbing will be well above his nostrils, just above where his hair changes colour, on the bony part of his face where it will not interfere with his breathing, but with

the side of the webbing well away from his eyes. If the halter is
going to be on for a little time or is going to be used to tie him up
you must make a knot where the rope comes through the loop so
that the noseband cannot pull too tight. If you find the headband is
too long it is easy to sew a tuck in it, but make sure it is firmly
sewn and cannot pull apart. Never resort to safety pins.

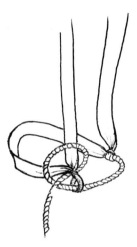

*A halter knotted so
that it cannot pull on
the donkey's nose.*

A **headcollar** is made on the same principle as a halter but the
strap that goes over his head (the headband) is permanently
fastened onto a band which goes round his nose, and an extra band
is attached from the sides which goes under his jaw and is kept
neatly in place by another strap joining it to the noseband under his
chin. To get it on and off it now has to have an opening, some
form of adjustable buckle, on the band at the side of his head.
Some headcollars also have a fastening on the noseband so that it
can be adjusted to fit.

Headcollars can be made from beautiful English leather with
brass buckles, or, these days, from strong nylon with rustproof
buckles which do not need cleaning. If you are going to parade
your donkey in public you may feel he would look smarter in a
leather headcollar, but a nylon one is strong and easy to keep clean
for home wear, and can be bought in various colours to suit his
beauty and your taste. Where the straps meet on the near side there
will be a ring where you attach a lead to handle him. This lead has

a clip on one end to attach it to the ring and it can be made of rope, in any colour to match his headcollar, a leather strap, or, if he is on show, a white leading rein which must be kept pristine.

The lead must be thick and it can have a knot at a strategic point near his headcollar to prevent it from slipping out of your hand. *Never* wind it round your hand (and this applies to the lead of a halter, too) in order to hold it more firmly. For safety you must be able to let go at once if it is necessary.

If you are taking him out on a leather headcollar he will look smarter with a browband that goes under his ears and across his forehead. It makes him look better dressed and shortens his face. This is usually bought separately and comes in various lengths to fit his forehead so that it neither hangs down his face nor pulls on his ears. You can get plain leather ones or choose from all kinds of patterns or colours.

You put on a headcollar exactly the same way as a halter, standing facing the same way as the donkey on his near side. This time you must unbuckle or loosen the strap that goes over the donkey's head, and, having slipped the noseband in place, you put the strap over the donkey's head and fasten the buckle to fit neatly. If it has a buckle on the noseband keep this closed until it is on the donkey and then adjust it to size. The noseband buckle on a headcollar always used for the same donkey will not need to be adjusted again.

Bridle If you are going to take a donkey onto a public road, unless he is so young and small that you are stronger than he is, he should be on a proper bridle and bit. It is impossible to hold an adult donkey on a headcollar if he is determined to get away, and, although he must be trained to do as he is told, should he be really frightened he will move quickly and suddenly and can pull away from you. Once he is loose he can injure himself or cause an unpleasant accident.

A bridle is like a headcollar where the straps are attached to a bit rather than a noseband; the bit goes through his mouth and is used for guiding him. Most bridles, however, have a noseband as well which comes down from the headband on separate straps. There is also a narrow strap which comes from the headband and goes under the donkey's throat and which is called a throat lash. This must be unbuckled every time the bridle is put on or off, and is never tight, but should allow you to put your four fingers comfortably between the strap and the donkey's neck.

The best bridles have all the straps adjustable on either side of his head so that you can make it fit perfectly.

The bit must fit well and be comfortable in the donkey's mouth. The most suitable kinds are a half-moon snaffle or a jointed snaffle. A half-moon bit is a straight bar of metal or nylon with a slight curve in it. A jointed bit has two pieces of metal joined in the middle. A snaffle bit describes one with quite large rings on either side which prevent the bit being pulled sideways through the donkey's mouth. A loop at the end of the bit goes through these rings and so do the straps from the headband; the reins are attached to the ring as well if he is being ridden or driven. When he is being led a strap or chain goes loosely under his chin and is attached to the two rings, and a leading rein is fastened to this.

When you are choosing a bit make sure it is a 'kind' one and not a bit designed to control a difficult horse, and that it fits well; it should not pinch the mouth but neither should it show too much at the sides. A 4½-inch bit is the right size for the average donkey, but yours might need a longer or a shorter one.

You put the bridle on in the same way as the halter and the headcollar, but this time you have the throat lash and the bit to manoeuvre as well. Undo the throat lash and loosen the head strap, then, once more standing on the near side of your donkey facing the same way as he does, you hold the bit in front of his mouth with your left hand, and the top of the bridle above his head with your right hand. Press your left thumb into the side of his mouth, where he has no teeth, gently open his mouth and slip in the bit, which goes in the toothless gap; then slide the headpiece over his ears.

Now adjust the head strap and fasten the throat lash. The bit should already be adjusted, but check that it is comfortable, with his mouth just slightly creased at the sides. If it is too loose it will hang down into his mouth and bang against his teeth so that it bothers him, and he will either get it under his tongue or hold it between his teeth, in which case you have no control over him at all. If it is too tight in the corners of his mouth he will think you are pulling on it all the time.

Keep all his tack clean. Nylon headcollars need to be washed from time to time and the buckles to be rubbed up. Leather tack should first be cleaned with a damp cloth to get dirt off and then treated with saddle soap. Saddle soap should be put on with a sponge *barely* wet — get this thoroughly filled with the soap and rub onto the leather. It should not leave any foam — wipe this off. Undo the buckles when you clean the tack and remember to soap the underside as well as the top. Polish the metal fittings, trying not to get the metal polish on the leather or on the bit. Keep the bit clean by washing it every time it is used with a clean piece of towelling and warm water — do not put detergent or anything else in the water.

You will find your donkey enjoys wearing his smart, clean tack.

9 Insurance

It is possible to insure your donkey against loss due to death and against veterinary fees. You can get the details of these policies from any of the equine insurance companies and you can decide whether you think it is worth while.

The insurance you *must* have is third-party liability. If your donkey escapes from his field, or is let out by vandals, and he strays into your neighbour's garden and damages it, or, much worse, he runs into the road and causes an accident, you are responsible; and it could cost you thousands of pounds in compensation. The Donkey Breed Society automatically covers all its members for third-party liability (it is worth joining for this alone) but if you are not a member you will probably be able to insure with the company that covers your house and contents — you may already be covered, but check with your insurance company. Do not procrastinate, but make sure your donkey is covered by insurance on arrival.

10 Grooming

Your donkey should have a little attention every day. If he is brushed all over, it not only keeps him clean and neat and discourages lice, but gives you an opportunity to notice small cuts, spots or bald patches. I do not mean that he must be groomed to show condition each day, but the loose hair and caked mud should be removed, his eyes should be kept clean and his hooves free from stones and mud.

You will need three brushes: a dandy brush, which has stiff bristles; a body brush, which is soft; and a brush with curved wire bristles which is sold for large dogs, and which you will find most useful of all during the winter months when his hair is thick. You will also need something to clean out his hooves; a hoof-pick is convenient for this, but they are sometimes unnecessarily sharply pointed, and a shaped piece of wood or hard plastic is safer, especially if you are dealing with a young donkey. You will also need some old clean towelling and hoof-oil.

To groom him, tie him to a post or ring and, facing towards his tail, start at the top of his head, and, using the wire brush, remove all the hayseed from his mane; hayseed can irritate him and make him rub, and even, if neglected, cause sores. Using whatever brush is most suitable, according to the season and the length of his hair, continue brushing down his neck, chest and side, smoothing the hair in its natural direction. Brush the outside of his near legs (you may need a softer brush for these) and the inside of those on his far side. Brush gently between his front legs and under his belly.

Lift his tail and hold it towards you along his side while you brush his back legs and rump, and then brush the tail itself, still held sideways towards you, being careful not to break any hairs.

When you have finished one side, walk round him and, still facing towards his tail, brush the other side in exactly the same way. It is correct to brush him from either side and never to stand directly behind him; I am not suggesting he would kick — I am sure he has perfect manners — but it is best to get into the habit of grooming the correct way. Brush his face and ears with a soft brush.

You will probably use the wire brush all over him during the winter, except for his face and ears, and perhaps his belly, and in the summer the dandy brush will take off the mud without scratching him, and will polish him up a bit. You will need the soft brush for his face and ears all the year round and it will make him shine all over in the summer when his coat is smooth.

Always keep his brushes clean and dust-free.

Most donkeys have a stiff upright mane and it looks smart if it is kept evenly trimmed. If he has a long mane, lift it and brush underneath it, then brush the mane out and encourage it to lie back all to the same side of his neck.

When you have finished brushing him lift each foot, always in the same order, and clean any mud or stones out of his hoof. Never let the mud harden round his feet and ankles. If you brush them every night they are unlikely to clog up. But if the mud gets too

Donkeys can have stiff upright manes like Kathleen's which need to be trimmed neatly.

Or they can have long manes like Moira's which should be encouraged to hang all to the same side.

solid to brush you will have to wash it off. Donkeys usually have no objection to putting one foot at a time into a bucket of tepid water but do not use any detergent or disinfectant in it; you can add salt if you think his ankles are slightly sore. Never try to pull the mud away or you will pull the hair off too; massage it gently until it melts away, then dry his legs and ankles thoroughly. If he is stabled at night in deep dry straw he is unlikely to be troubled by mud as his feet will have time to dry out.

Once a week give him a special groom and brush him until he shines, getting most of the dust out of his coat. Wipe out the insides of his ears with a soft cloth, but be careful not to probe down too far into his ears. Some donkeys make rather a lot of soft wax which hangs on the tufts of hair that grow on the inside of their ears and this should be gently teased out. I hate to see donkeys with clots of wax hanging from their ears, it gives them a neglected look.

Also make sure, at least weekly, that the corners of his eyes and his nostrils are free from dust or mucus, using a clean cloth and tepid water to which a little salt has been added. Again, do not use any detergent, antiseptic or disinfectant. If he needs washing at the back under his tail make sure you use the cloth on his face *first*. Check his feet more thoroughly once a week and paint his hooves with hoof oil.

Donkeys are naturally clean and rather vain creatures, and they appreciate looking their best — a well groomed animal will carry himself with more confidence.

11 *Exercise*

To keep any animal fit and healthy it must be encouraged to take some exercise every day. The amount a donkey needs depends on his age and to some extent on the food you are giving him.

A working donkey who drives or is ridden regularly, or a show donkey who is trained to trot round the ring on command, will get all the exercise he needs. If you have two donkeys in a paddock of over half an acre they will exercise each other; young donkeys play together incessantly, standing on their back legs and pretending to bite each other's necks, and chasing round the field together.

(Opposite) *Marius and Menier playing together when they were two-year-old colts. Donkeys' play might look rough, but if the animals have a good temperament they are careful not to hurt each other. When examined that evening both animals were unmarked.*

Older donkeys too, if there is more than one, will have a good canter round the field, kicking their heels in all directions and taking it in turns to be leader. Even elderly donkeys will feel the urge to play on certain days and circle the field holding their heads sideways and demonstrating that they are still capable of their lovely extended trot and watching you to make sure you are applauding them.

However, one donkey, especially if he is kept in a small paddock, will need to be exercised or he will get bored and fat and possibly troublesome. To be taken for a walk would not only exercise him but give him a chance to see something of the outside world and learn to meet people, dogs and other animals. He would enjoy being taken to your local shop wearing panniers and would help you carry your shopping home. Everyone will speak to him and he will have a lovely time.

He would love to accompany the family on a picnic, carrying the food for you and finding some new and interesting browsing for himself — but do watch him and make sure he cannot reach any poisonous plant or tree.

Donkeys can be taught to be lunged. Lunging is what we see going on at horse shows, where a single rein is attached to a horse's bridle and he is made to circle at a walk, trot or a canter and halt at the word of command. By this means an animal may be exercised without the necessity of carrying a rider or pulling a cart and without too much labour on the part of the handler. Unfortunately this does not come naturally to a donkey whose policy is to walk straight towards his owner to exchange affectionate greetings. Therefore it is necessary at first to have two people, one to stand in the centre of the circle and give instructions and the other to hold his head and keep him moving on the correct path.

Lunging certainly exercises satisfactorily and moreover would give you the feeling of accomplishment once he is trained.

12 *Training*

To most of us it seems obvious that an animal should be trained to do as it is told and to have good manners, whether you intend to take him out and show him or keep him as a pet. Donkeys are intelligent and training is a means of putting their intelligence to good use. Yet I know there are some people who feel that training is unnecessary and say, 'Why should he learn to wear a halter or learn to be tied up if he doesn't like it? I just want him to be happy. What does it matter if he won't walk or trot when I tell him?'

My reply would be that it could matter quite a lot in an emergency. Just suppose his stable caught fire: would he stand still and let you slip a halter over his head on the command of 'stand'? Would he lead out when you asked and would he let you tie him up outside while you returned for his companion?

Quite apart from safety, I believe a donkey likes to be trained. He enjoys it because you are with him, giving him your attention, and because it fills an instinctive need: donkeys are herd animals and in his wild state your donkey would accept without question the discipline imposed by the leader of the herd. In his domestic state the donkey will regard you as his leader and will accept the discipline you impose upon him in the form of training. Indeed he will expect it, and if you are unable or unwilling to assert your authority he will challenge your leadership by doing as he likes, and trying to make you do what he wants.

When I talk about asserting authority I am not suggesting you should dominate him; what his training should accomplish is a partnership in which you are the leader, using your superior intelligence to develop and utilize his lesser, but adequate, intelligence. Such a partnership must be based on mutual trust, respect and affection.

There is another aspect: a donkey has a life-span of thirty or even forty years and you might not be able to have him with you all his life; indeed, he could change hands several times. If he is well trained he will, without doubt, have a happier life with his new owners, should you have to part with him. A well behaved donkey will always make friends and be treated with respect. But what of an untrained donkey? His new owners *might,* we hope, have the knowledge and patience to begin training him. But they might find him too difficult and pass him on to someone else who just considered him stupid, stubborn and badly behaved, and whose idea of training included a lot of shouting and whacking.

Once he is trained you can take him to shows (which donkeys adore) or he can go for walks with the family, can carry your shopping and take part in the local fêtes and nativity plays, raise funds for charity and so on.

An untrained donkey can do nothing but stay in his field or his stable.

Of course you may be fortunate enough to acquire a donkey who has already been fully trained and he will be a joy. But do find out if possible the command words that were used by his previous owner. If you are interested in training him further you can always consider long-reining, even if you do not intend to drive him, or you could get him so accomplished at navigating obstacles he would win every handy donkey class at shows.

The lessons an untrained donkey must learn are to walk and trot when told. To stand still. To walk backwards and move sideways. To allow himself to be tied up to a post or ring inside or outside his stable. To allow all his feet to be lifted (though not at once: we had a young colt, Adam, who was so keen to oblige that when you lifted one foot he would lift another, usually falling on his face). He will need to learn to walk into a stable or horsebox on command, and to stand still in the stable or box when the door is opened instead of pushing out past you. He will also need to learn how to move and stand while you open and close a gate, and he must be able to meet other animals without being either aggressive or timid.

When you first get your donkey home he has got to get to know and respect you. Spend as much time as possible with him and talk to him all the time so that he gets to know your voice. The first words he must learn are 'Good boy' when you are pleased with him and 'No!' if he is being naughty — or whatever words you choose to express your praise and condemnation. If you know what words his last owners used of course you must stick to these, but if he has to learn new words it does not matter what they are provided they are easily differentiated and you always stick to the same ones. When you are pleased with him do not just say 'Good boy' but

A donkey must learn to stand still when told. Justavius at two.

sound pleased and affectionate. If you have to correct him (perhaps he has caught your shirt between his teeth, which is really a loving gesture but cannot be allowed) say 'No!' firmly, sounding displeased, as you withdraw your shirt from his mouth. Then if he keeps his mouth closed for the next minute tell him in a pleased and loving voice that he is a 'Good boy!'

Never shout at him, it will frighten and confuse him. Donkeys will usually do what you want them to if they understand what is required and know you are determined to be obeyed. If they realize you will get your way in the end they will consider it easier to do as you say and not to have all that fuss, but beware of them getting to

enjoy the fuss, and do not keep using tit-bits to teach them; they
are clever enough to know that if they refuse to obey you at first
they are more likely to be bribed. If you watch a mare correcting a
foal when he has been naughty you will see that she usually bites
him on the top of his front legs. He knows this means he has been
badly behaved, but it obviously causes no pain and he appears to
feel no resentment; so it is better for us to slap a donkey on his
chest if he pulls our clothes, or even nips, than to slap his nose,
which will only result in him approaching you with his nose up in
the air, or not coming to you at all.

The other way a donkey can hurt you is by throwing up his heels
in sheer *joie de vivre* without noticing you are standing behind him.
I think this is more difficult to correct as he is not doing anything
wrong, it is only his timing which is at fault. You will have to
dodge his heels and hope your command of 'No!' penetrates. It
helps if you always talk to him and put your hand on his rump
when you are behind him.

If your donkey ever kicks at you on purpose he will require a
really strong reprimand and if you are able to catch him across the
kicking leg with the end of a rope or a stick while he is actually
kicking, so much the better. It is useless to punish him five
minutes, or even five seconds, later as he will not understand what
you are cross about. Fortunately donkeys seldom kick maliciously
unless they have been ill treated, and have needed to defend
themselves, in the past.

To start your donkey's training, put on his halter or headcollar
and stand at his near side, slightly behind his head, with your right
hand holding the lead rein and actually touching his cheek, keeping
your wrist stiff so that you have him under complete control. Point
him in the direction you think he would like to go (possibly towards
a bowl with a few ponynuts in it which you have placed a little
distance away) and push him gently forward with your stiff arm
saying 'Walk - walk - walk'. If he moves forward continue to say
'Walk' so that he associates the word with moving forward, with a
'Good boy' thrown in now and again to show he is pleasing you. If
he breaks into a trot change the word to 'Trot' and if he stops say
'Stand' until he moves again. When he gets to the bowl let him eat
the nuts (three or four are enough) and start all over again. When
you have been teaching him the words for some time you can start

to ask him to walk, trot and stand at your command instead of his choice.

Never at any time get in front of him and pull him to make him go: always push him with a stiff wrist from his shoulder. If he stops and you get in front of him you must stop too and go back to the correct position behind his shoulder.

You will easily learn to carry a stick in your left hand — a bamboo cane is excellent — and if he refuses to walk on command put the stick behind your back and tap him on the rump. The idea is not to hurt him, but to prompt him from the back.

Keep his training short for the first few times — ten minutes is enough to begin with, and always try to finish when you are pleased with him and he is doing the right thing so that the correct procedure remains in his memory. You can lengthen the time you

A donkey being led under the 'line of washing' in Heathfield Versatile Donkey Class: one of the times a donkey needs to be led from the front of his head.

spend training after a few days, but you will find several short sessions remain in his mind better than one longer one. If you feel you are getting frustrated or might lose your temper (and all donkeys can be trying at times), give up at once: you will do no good. It takes concentration on your part because you must will him and expect him to do as you want. If either of you is getting bored leave his training till the next day.

Once he has learnt to stand on command he can be taught to be tied up. Again, take it slowly. Make sure the post or ring you tie him to is rock solid so that he cannot feel he is making it move. Stand him beside it telling him to 'Stand', then tie him up with a slip knot, and stay beside him talking to him for a few minutes before releasing him. Each time leave him tied up a little longer. If he struggles to get away hold him by his halter and make him stand calmly while you are holding him before you untie him: never let him get the idea that struggling will get him loose.

Once he seems to be happy when tied up try giving him a small net of hay and leaving him briefly, secretly keeping an eye on him to make sure he does not miss you and panic.

Unless he learns to stand still and have his feet picked up you will have difficulty in getting a farrier to trim his hooves; if a farrier has to use force, foot trimming will become frightening for him. You have already started training him to have his feet lifted when you are grooming him; now, if he has not learnt to be tied up yet, you will need a helper to hold his head. Stand close beside him, facing his rump, and slowly run your hand down his front leg from his shoulder. When your hand reaches his hoof say 'Up' and pick it up. Soon he will learn to pick it up for you. Replace his foot on the ground saying 'Down' before he thinks of kicking it out of your hand. At first only hold his foot for a moment, and do not lift it too high. Next time tap his sole before putting it down. You will find he learns quickly and if you support his foot a little longer each time and sometimes tap it before putting it down he will gradually accept it as a routine. Go round the four legs in the same order each time.

If he does start to struggle and kick with a back leg before you have put it down I am afraid you must hang on and put it down yourself. Try to hold his foot gently, as he kicks it backwards and forwards, without tightening your grip on his ankle so that you frighten or even hurt him. If he once discovers that he can kick his foot out of your control you will be in trouble. Always put his foot down on the ground — never just drop it.

Once he has learnt to walk forwards willingly at your command you can start training him to move backwards by putting your left hand flat on his chest and gently but firmly pushing him backwards while repeating the word 'Back'. Eventually he should move backwards without having to be pushed, but it takes time. Never let him graze or snatch mouthfuls of grass while he is being trained — he must give you his full attention.

If he is unused to traffic let him examine your car and walk round it while it is parked, then get him accustomed to it with the engine running and finally when it is moving.

If you have a trailer or horsebox make sure he will load and unload without fuss. Should he be frightened to walk up the ramp, and, after all, his few previous experiences may not have been pleasant by far the easiest way of getting him used to a trailer is to park it in his paddock with a net of hay and a small bowl of ponynuts inside and leave him alone. Curiosity and greed will win and once he will go in and out on his own he will allow you to lead him up the ramp.

One of the best ways of getting him used to travelling, strangers, noise and meeting other animals is to take him to a local show. He will love it and you will be delighted to discover how friendly other donkey owners are. Chapter 14 is about showing.

When he knows you, and will walk on command, try taking him up steps and slopes and through narrow doorways. He should trust you enough to go anywhere you tell him. A donkey taking part in a nativity play has to face countless hazards: ours have walked up flights of steps, squeezed through heavy curtains into darkened porches, and crossed hissing heating grilles; Barnabas has trotted briskly down a narrow slippery aisle during the Flight to Egypt and manoeuvred a tight turn round the back pew. We have had slight mishaps, as when Kathleen nibbled the straw in the manger, but they seem to be forgiven. It was Kathleen, too, who, when turned away from the Inn (which was a local hostelry) lifted up her voice and drowned the carol.

A very old donkey can be difficult to train as he will have become set in his ways, and you may not know what words of

Kathleen is taking part in the Nativity at Mayfield in Sussex where the Holy Family with angels and choirs used to walk up the village street asking for shelter at various inns.

command have been used in the past. Take your time with him, and remember he may have had some unpleasant experiences in life. Until you know an elderly donkey well do not take liberties with him; he may be reminded of something in his earlier life which will make him react by biting or kicking.

Some time during your donkey's training you are almost certain to become disheartened, but suddenly everything will come right for you both, and a well mannered donkey is a joy to himself, his owner and everybody he meets.

13 *Carrying, Riding and Driving*

PANNIERS

Donkeys have been used as pack animals since they were first domesticated and one of the simplest methods of arranging weight evenly on their backs is to have a basket or bag of some kind hanging on either side of the animal. In those countries where donkeys are used regularly as pack animals a most elaborate harness is used; often a frame made from wood fits across the back, which must add considerably to the load.

If you simply put a strap from pannier to pannier over the back

Titania's owner, Virginia Heaton, made these basket-work panniers. They are fitted to a driving pad.

of the donkey, all the weight would be taken on one point of his backbone, which would soon become sore and even damaged, so a pad must be devised to take the weight off his bone and spread it evenly over his back. The pad from a driving harness is ideal as it is designed for the purpose of spreading weight and has a girth strap and a crupper to hold it in place (a crupper is a strap which goes from the back of the pad and passes round the donkey's tail), but a felt saddle works well with the bags or baskets held by the stirrup bars, and has the advantage that it protects his sides from being rubbed or bumped. A saddle, too, will need a crupper, and in either case you must make sure it is comfortable and the girth does not rub his front legs.

If you have neither driving pad nor saddle and he is only going to wear the panniers for a short time, and will not be carrying much weight, you could put a thick pad made from an old blanket over his back, folded so that it is thicker at the edges than in the middle and so takes the weight off his backbone, and strap it round his body — you must use a wide strap, not less than three inches, or it will cut him. You can hang baskets or bags across this, making sure they will not bump uncomfortably against his sides.

RIDING

A donkey does not need to be broken. I have never known one to object to having a small child lifted on to his back and held while he is being led. If they encounter a rider whom they consider too heavy, or to be taking advantage of them in some way, however, they are adept at removing the rider, either by bucking, bending one leg so that they slither off, or as a last resort brushing them off under a low branch; but they would never do this with a small child. Being warm and woolly, and slow movers, they exude confidence to nervous little riders, but if you are lifting a tiny child onto a donkey's back it is best to have a second person to attend to the donkey while you look after the child. If possible put a strap or belt round the donkey's neck for the child to hold on to, otherwise tell it to hold the hair at the base of the mane; never let a child hold on by the reins, which would pull on the donkey's mouth.

Older children who are past the stage of being held on will get much more pleasure from riding a donkey if he is trained and the rider is taught by a qualified person. Eight stone is the maximum weight which should be carried by a 10 -hand donkey, and as he matures more slowly than a horse he must not be ridden until he is four years old.

An older rider will need a saddle for riding and the usual snaffle bridle, with reins attached to the rings at the side of the donkey's face. A felt saddle is most suitable for a donkey, and more easily fitted than a leather one, but you must make sure the girth strap does not rub the donkey's forelegs and it must have a well fitted crupper or the saddle will slide forwards onto the donkey's neck.

Make sure the stirrup leathers are attached to safety bars so that the leathers will come away from the saddle should the rider fall off, and the stirrups must fit correctly: big enough to let the rider's boots slide out easily but not so large that she can get her foot caught through the stirrups (I am presuming the rider is a girl only to distinguish her easily from the donkey). If the rider is a novice there should be a strap on the front of the saddle for her to hold if she is nervous; never let her balance by holding the reins tightly.

Most donkeys will accept a rider without any training. Let one person hold the donkey while another, not too heavy, person leans across his back, eventually taking their feet off the ground. If the donkey has no objection to this place the saddle on his back, still having his head held by a second handler, and if he accepts it fasten the girth slowly, keeping it fairly loose until he is used to it. Then walk him about a little. Depending on the time he takes to accept the saddle, the next stage is to gently tighten the girth, talking to him all the time, and attach the crupper and the stirrup leathers. He may object more to having the crupper put round his tail than having the saddle on his back. Make sure it is comfortable, and is soft and does not rub under his tail.

Once he is used to the saddle, crupper and stirrups lean once again across his back to make sure it does not make him nervous and, when you are confident all is well, lift the rider into the saddle, holding her while the other handler leads the donkey. Do not let her mount by using the stirrup the first time she is on his back unless she is an experienced rider and be ready to lift her off quickly if the donkey is being troublesome.

The riding position and aids are exactly the same as for a pony and any good book on riding will give detailed instructions. Your donkey will already be trained to walk, trot and move backwards,

The winner of a Heathfield riding class on Katherina of Harbolets, owned by Mrs Ann Jones.

and, most important of all, to stand still, and the rider can start by using these words until the donkey has learnt to connect the words with the rider's movements.

To mount a donkey the rider should stand at the near side (the donkey's left side), hold the reins in her left hand and with the same hand hold the front of the saddle. She then puts her left foot in the stirrup and swings her right leg over the saddle, putting her right foot in the other stirrup.

She should hold the reins in such a way that she can just feel the donkey's mouth. To make the donkey move forward she says, 'Walk on', or whatever words have been used during training, and

A very small child sitting on Teena's back and balancing without the help of saddle or reins.

slightly loosens the reins, leans forward a little and squeezes with her legs. Try to preeent her from flapping her legs and kicking at the donkey if he does not obey at once; it looks so awful and will only confuse him.

To turn right she should shorten the right rein and squeeze with her right leg, and to turn left she does exactly the opposite.

To halt she must pull *gently* on the reins and once again squeeze slightly with her legs while giving the appropriate instructions.

It is important that she learns how to dismount safely: she must hold both reins in her left hand at the front of the saddle and take *both* feet out of the stirrups, then swing her right leg over the donkey's back and slip down to the ground with both feet at the same time. She must *always* take her left foot out of the stirrup at the same time as her right foot so that she cannot get left with one foot on the ground and one in a stirrup which could be extremely dangerous if the donkey started to move. She should still be holding her reins in her left hand over the donkey's neck.

This is most elementary; to get pleasure from riding, an older child should be taught by an experienced rider. Donkeys can become a reasonably good mount if well trained, can be used for gymkhana classes, and can be taught to jump; at the 5th D.B.S. Championship Show Cleone Kingsley-Lewis gave a dressage display on her 11-hand donkey who she hunted regularly with the Cambridgeshire Harriers.

DRIVING

It is impossible to tell anyone how to ride a donkey without writing an entire book on the subject, and driving a donkey is even more skilled, but perhaps I can help you to set about obtaining the knowledge without making too many expensive mistakes.

The Donkey Breed Society is, as always, your first source of information. There is an enthusiastic Driving Section which will give you tremendous help in the form of literature and practical demonstrations. There will almost certainly be a member living near you who can help you train your donkey, tell you where to buy a suitable harness locally and how to find a vehicle which fits him.

Donkeys drive well and usually enjoy being driven, but it is a skilled art and both driver and donkey must be trained before he is taken onto a public road; it is more difficult to control an animal from the driving position than it is when you are walking beside him or riding him. Most donkeys are easy to break to harness — in fact 'break' is an unpleasant and unsuitable word: all that is needed is to get him accustomed to wearing the harness and pulling a vehicle and trained to respond to your instructions. The training you have already been giving him is a splendid foundation to driving.

It is not easy to get a harness to fit a donkey well as it is usually made for a pony, and a donkey is a slightly different shape, so it may be necessary to have some small alterations made by a saddler. If you intend to use your donkey for driving locally, collecting logs

Virginia Heaton driving Oberon. Mrs Heaton and Oberon won the D.B.S. Driving Championship in 1980.

and transporting straw and hay from barn to stable, exercise harness made principally of webbing will be satisfactory and easy to keep clean.

Donkeys, these days, usually have a breast harness — the old-fashioned full neck collars which we see donkeys wearing in pictures of asses and carts in Ireland are clumsy and difficult to fit perfectly. The breast collar is easy to fit: it should be broad to take the weight evenly, and must be neither too high, where it will catch his windpipe, or so low that it rubs his shoulders. The pad, which goes on his back and takes the weight of the cart on the straps down to the tugs on the shafts, might need extra padding to keep it from resting on his spine if your donkey has a rather 'sharp' backbone, and the crupper may need to be lengthened because donkeys' tails are usually set slightly lower than ponies' tails. Donkeys are often slimmer than ponies, too, and the girth might need to be shortened.

The cart must fit the donkey and it is not always easy to find one small enough. Any light two-wheeled exercise cart will do, but it must be sound and safe. The late Dr Marcus Campbell made his carts himself, for singles, pairs and tandem (one donkey in front of the other) and used to show with much success. A rough guide to the size of the vehicle is that the bottom of the cart and the shafts should be parallel to the ground and the shafts should come about halfway up the donkey's sides and must not extend too far beyond him in front.

To train him, put his harness on slowly, talking to him, and when he seems relaxed walk him about, leading him from the head and using the normal words of command. Then try him on long reins, which means driving him from behind with the reins extended, using your voice and the reins to make him start, trot, turn to right and left and stop, and to stand still always until commanded to move. He should also walk backwards when asked. Before putting him to the cart, tie a piece of wood to both ends of the traces and see if he objects to pulling a weight. If he takes to all this happily, and most donkeys do, you can harness him up; it is safer at this stage to have two people, one to hold the donkey at his head and the other to fit the harness to the cart. Back him between the shafts, lift them up a little and lower them into the tugs; fasten the traces and do up the girth and the breeching (the strap which goes loosely round behind him to prevent the cart running forward when he is going down hill), adjusting it so that it hangs 3 or 4 inches behind his hindquarters.

Walk him forward slowly with a person on either side of his head — he may take time to get used to the feel of the shafts along his sides. Next have one person at his head while the other drives from the ground behind him, and when you feel he is safe, get into the cart to drive, but always have an assistant at his head until you are confident of his behaviour. Make sure he is not frightened when you drive downhill and the breeching comes forward onto his body, and that he will always stand perfectly still and not move off until told.

When you are taking him out of the vehicle it is important to remember that the *last* thing to do is to take off his bridle.

You may find it takes a few weeks to progress to this stage; on the other hand donkeys have been known to drive satisfactorily on their first afternoon.

If you intend to drive him at shows his harness and cart become much more complicated. To begin with he must have a proper driving bridle with blinkers (which might take some getting used to — and should be fitted properly) and not only the quality of harness and cart, but the correct colour of harness for each type of vehicle, the handling of the whip (which must be held in the right hand and never left in the socket) and even such things as your own dress and the candles in the lamps are assessed, although there are some shows which put on classes to judge the skill of the donkey and driver in exercise carts.

As well as show classes for donkeys, the Driving Section of the D.B.S. organizes all kinds of 'open days', demonstrations and drives and picnics in the country; driving your donkey is one of the best ways of enjoying your donkey while giving him pleasure and needed exercise.

14 Showing

Showing is tremendous fun for both the donkey and his owner. You will meet all the other owners, who will be happy to make friends with a new donkey lover, and your animal will have an interesting time watching and talking to new acquaintances, both human and equine.

When the Donkey Breed Society was first formed to improve the welfare of donkeys, it was decided that we needed a shop window to let the general public see how a really well kept donkey should look and to encourage all donkey owners to keep their animals in the best possible health and condition. In those days, over twenty years ago, many donkeys were neglected and badly cared-for through the ignorance of their owners. At the first shows the exhibitors were constantly greeted with the words, 'I never knew a donkey could look like that! How do you do it?'

A number of eminent horse and pony judges were persuaded to become donkey judges, and many shows, including some important county shows, introduced classes for donkeys. Soon shows were put on for donkeys only, and in 1970 the D.B.S. organized its first Championship Show at the National Equestrian Centre, Stoneleigh, with twenty-eight classes and Richard Baker to present the trophies.

Find out which local shows include donkeys and send for their schedules to see which classes your donkey is eligible for, not forgetting that his age is calculated from January 1st of the year in which he was born.

If he has not been shown before he will certainly qualify for the Novice Class (a class for a donkey who has not won a first prize in any in-hand, i.e. being led, show) and for one other breed class either for youngstock or adult donkeys. There is often a class for owners who have only two or three donkeys, the idea being to eliminate the large showing studs and give the private owners a better chance. There is also sometimes a class for Condition and Turnout, when the donkeys are judged on their health and immaculacy of donkey and tack and not on their conformation.

Sometimes there are non-breed classes, such as Driving, Children's Riding or perhaps an Obstacle Race, often called a 'Versatile Donkey' class, in which the donkey is led by you or a volunteer and has to negotiate various obstacles as quickly as possible. Decide which classes you can enter and send off your entry form in good time, then start to prepare your donkey, both for presentation and shining condition.

Start brushing him more thoroughly every day to get out any loose hair and bring up the shine on his coat. Have his hooves specially pared (it is better to have this done a week before the show so that he is walking comfortably on the day) and make sure you have the right bridle or headcollar to show him on and either a leather strap to handle him or a clean white leading rein.

A donkey usually shows better on a bridle with a bit than he does on a headcollar — you have more control of him and he will hold his head better. However, if you are showing a mare or gelding you are allowed to show them on a headcollar provided you are able to control them satisfactorily. All stallions and colts of three years or over must be bitted.

Start giving him extra training at once. He will need to walk on

Miss Marjorie Dunkels judging the stallion and gelding class at Halland Horse Show.

command in a straight line — a brisk walk shows him off better — and turn and trot back, once again in a straight line. He must always turn right so that he is on the inside and you push him round with your right arm, otherwise you will get between him and the judge. Above all he must stand still when told. You will have taught him to stand beside you, but he needs to 'stand out' to show himself off. This means standing evenly with all his legs straight and his head and ears held well up. If he rests one leg the trick is to push him slightly backwards until he straightens himself out; you and he will get the knack quite easily.

Arrange for transport. If you have your own trailer make sure he walks in and out without hesitating. If you have to hire a horsebox and driver the driver will help you load him.

The day before the show give his bridle a special polish making sure it is clean on the underside (especially if you are entering the Best Condition and Turnout) and make the buckles gleam. Check that his leading rein is clean and have a headcollar or ready knotted halter for him to wear when he is travelling and while he is waiting for his class at the show.

You will need to take a grooming kit with you to touch him up before he goes into the ring, a damp cloth in a plastic bag to clean off any unexpected stains, and a clean towel to dry him again. You will also need a net of hay for him to nibble at the show and some water if it is going to be a long day.

Now tie up your donkey and get every speck of dust out of his coat. Some people shampoo their donkeys, but we never do, even in the height of summer, as we are sure most donkeys dislike it and it is bad to take the natural oil out of their coats. We use an

Hadrian, owned by Kim Parrish, standing out well at Halland Horse show.

ordinary household cylinder vacuum cleaner with the upholstery attachment, but it is possible to buy a special vacuum grooming kit. If you are going to use a vacuum cleaner get him used to it well before the show, keeping the cylinder away from him and letting him see and hear it switched on before you start to groom him.

The best way of all is to brush and keep on brushing. If he has any stains, wash them off with warm water and a not too strong soap, or a cattle or equine shampoo. Wash his tail by dipping it into a bucket of soapy water; dry and comb it well out to make the most of it. If it is straggly at the end, trim it discreetly, trying to leave it as long as possible; personally I do not like to see donkeys' tails cut straight across — they should look natural. Wash his eyes and nose gently with tepid water. Pick out his feet carefully and wash and dry them if they are muddy, then paint with hoof-oil — you will need to clean and paint them again after you arrive at the show.

If he has an upright mane it is sure to need trimming; this is quite an art, and it is best just to straighten the tufts until you acquire the necessary skill. Some people cut away all the donkey-coloured hair on either side of the mane leaving only the stiff black hairs but I do not like this as it can make your donkey appear to have a weak neck, and if your scissors slip it can mean disaster. When you are using a pair of scissors on a donkey you must always make sure they have rounded ends. When you are satisfied with his appearance shut him in for the night with his usual food and keep him in until you are ready to set off in the morning. If you let him out he will certainly roll in any mud or dust he can find.

When he is travelling to the show do not tie him up or he can hurt himself if he slips. He will stand and balance with his rump in a corner and facing backwards. He must wear a headcollar or knotted halter with the rope tied back across the top of his neck so that it cannot choke him, so that you can catch him easily in an emergency. Get to the show at least an hour before his class is due and give him a few minutes in his box or trailer to get his balance before unloading him. Once he is out, walk him round before tying him up to the side of the box. He may be excited, and if so walk him until he calms down, talking to him and trying to keep him away from other donkeys or horses.

You may have to collect your numbers from the secretary's tent if they have not been sent to you. If so try to stay with your donkey as it is his first show and send somebody else to fetch his number while you give him a final groom, wash and dry any stains he has picked up during the night, clean and put hoof-oil on his feet and put on his bridle. Put back his halter or headcollar on top of the bridle and tie him up by that; never tie him up by his bridle.

When you are both tidy put his number on your back or left arm, depending on the length of string provided, take him to the collecting ring about ten minutes before the class is due to start and walk him about to keep him interested. Never feed him at the show before he goes into the ring, he does not need it, neither will he need water until he finishes showing. Do not let him eat grass, either while he is tied up before his class or while he is walking about with his bridle on. Once he has finished showing and you have taken off his bridle you can lengthen the lead of his halter so that he is able to graze, always provided the grass looks clean and wholesome and has not been trampled and soiled. You must stay with him while he is on a long rope or he will certainly get tangled up. If the grass is unappetizing tie a net of hay for him to nibble.

IN THE RING

The usual procedure in a donkey class is as follows: the donkeys go into the ring and walk round in a clockwise direction, with the judge in the middle of the ring. You will not want to be the first in the ring so follow another donkey, keeping well away from him; you will be unpopular with his handler if you get too close to the animal in front as it will distract him and prevent him from showing himself off properly. You walk in a clockwise direction because your donkey is held on his near side and the judge wants to see him and not you. Make him walk briskly, if possible looking alert with his ears up. If you find you are catching up with a slower donkey in front enlarge your ring so that you are able to take him at the pace you like. The judge may ask you all to trot, either one at a time or together.

The judge then asks her steward to 'pull in' the donkeys in what she now believes to be the order of merit. She has not seen them at close quarters yet so this will probably not be the final order. Watch the steward, and when she calls you, take your donkey into the centre of the ring and stand him in line in the place indicated. He must stand as well as possible all the time he is in the ring and look his best always, not only when the judge is examining him, because she will be comparing the donkeys when you least expect it.

She may walk down the line first having a closer look at all the animals or she may call them out to her straight away, starting with the donkey she called in first. Unless you are at the top of the line you will have a chance to watch the other competitors and see what they do, but never stop concentrating on how your donkey is standing, and above all discourage your next-door neighbours from chatting to you.

When called, you walk your donkey to the judge and stand him squarely in front of her making him look as handsome as possible — make sure he is not resting one leg. The judge will examine him from all sides and may ask some questions; she may want to know his age, or if you have a mare she may ask if she is in foal or if she has had any foals. Then she will indicate to you to walk him away from her, turn and trot him back again. Walk straight and turn him to the right so that he is between you and the judge — you have been practising this — then trot him back in as straight a line as possible. If the judge stands immediately in front of you, so that you fear you may run her down, keep straight ahead at her: she is looking to see how he moves and she cannot see his action if you are both weaving from side to side. Don't worry, she will get out of the way in time. When you reach the end of the line of donkeys you continue round behind them and back to your own place. If your donkey gets stage fright and refuses to trot, or even to move at all, please do not worry; it has happened to all of us and you will have the sympathy and good wishes of every other exhibitor. Make sure you never get in front of him and pull him, but stay behind at his shoulder and push with a stiff arm.

When the donkeys have done their 'show' they walk round again in the same direction as before and the judge asks the steward to call them in for what is usually their final placing. She has now seen the donkeys from the back and front as well as the side and has seen their action, so she may alter the order in which she first chose them. If your donkey has walked and trotted straight and freely he has a good chance of being put in front of one who has been pulled or has trotted badly.

A donkey refusing to show her paces during a Versatile Donkey class.

The judge will now walk down the line presenting the rosettes to the winners and probably having a word with other competitors. We have one delightful judge who gives any donkey who has not won a rosette a peppermint — I sometimes wonder if any animal is intelligent enough to make sure he gets into the 'peppermint syndrome' instead of winning a rosette.

Even if you are at the bottom of the line you must look happy and pleased. Do not speak to the judge while you are in the ring unless you are spoken to: it is no good telling her that he always trots at home, or that he was placed top of the line at another show last week. This is her choice; she has given up time and expended energy to come and judge the donkeys. If you are fortunate enough to win a rosette thank the judge when it is handed to you and fasten it to the off (right) side of your donkey's bridle.

It is good manners to dress appropriately. Riding clothes are excellent for horse owners, but a woman can wear any neat skirt or slacks, preferably with a jacket, but if not with a clean shirt or pullover. A simple cotton dress is acceptable in summer at a local show. You should look neat and inconspicuous, and your hair should be tidy and controlled. Sun-tops and scruffy jeans are definitely bad manners. Shoes should be flat-heeled and strong enough to withstand being trodden on by a donkey; sandals are not suitable. Men must be tidy and should wear a jacket and collar and tie. At the larger or county shows women should also wear a jacket and if possible a simple hat, and men should wear a hat which can be doffed to the judge when appropriate.

I think I can promise you that each time you go to a show you will enjoy it more. You will find the other donkey exhibitors friendly and helpful, especially if you tell them you have just started showing, and you will enjoy discussing donkeys together.

15 Teeth

As with a horse, a donkey's age can be told from his teeth, at least until he is ten years old. After that he is referred to as 'aged' which is a calumny, as he is in the prime of life. With experience you can get a good idea of a donkey's age from the teeth until he is well into his late twenties and really is becoming aged.

A foal gets his first front teeth within three or four days of his birth. Apparently they do not give him any trouble coming through but he may nibble the fence. By the time he is two years old he will have a full set of milk, or first teeth. Gradually, usually starting when he is about two and a half, these are replaced by permanent teeth, and the shape of his face alters. By the time he is five years old he will have a complete set of teeth.

Donkey teeth have to first bite off, then grind, all their food, which is frequently dry and hard, down to a suitable consistency to be digested, so they are given heavy use. Unlike ours they keep growing throughout the donkey's life; so as they wear down, they are renewed. This is splendid in theory but not always so efficient in practice and if you look in the mouth of a very old donkey you may find he has long teeth ('a bit long in the tooth') sloping outwards from his jaw, but more often that he has practically no teeth at all. Sometimes one set of teeth will grow and the other almost disappear.

The teeth of an elderly donkey with the top teeth worn almost down to the gums.

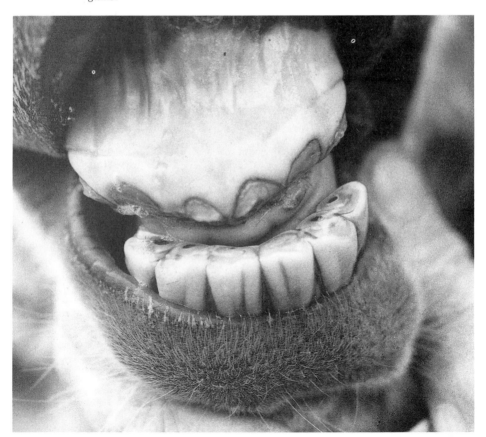

Teeth meeting perfectly.

An overshot jaw (parrot mouth).

An undershot jaw.

His teeth can start wearing unevenly from an early age, especially if they do not meet accurately. A donkey's teeth should meet exactly in the front if you pull back his lips when his teeth are closed. A little variation is allowed in the show ring but one edge of his top teeth must meet the other edge of his lower teeth. If the front teeth overlap the lower ones it is known as 'overshot' or 'parrot mouth' and as 'undershot' if the bottom teeth are in front. It is a hereditary fault and is forbidden in the Donkey Breed Society Stud Book.

When his teeth overlap in front, all his teeth, including his molars at the back, will be slightly out of alignment, and this will mean that when he grinds them together, eating his food, they will not match, and sharp edges and spikes will develop on the edges of his teeth. These can cut the donkey's tongue or, more often, the insides of his cheeks, or they can prevent his teeth from meeting so that he is not grinding his food sufficiently for him to digest it efficiently.

If your donkey seems to have any eating problems; if he approaches his food with enthusiasm then turns away, rolls his food round in his mouth, dribbles some out again, or if you ever find unchewed wedges of food in his cheek — indeed, if you get the impression in any way that he is not happy when he is eating, get your veterinary surgeon to check his teeth. Although this is mainly a problem with older donkeys, they can start having sharp edges on their teeth when they are quite young, and it is best to have their teeth examined each year.

If the teeth need to be filed it is a simple procedure: the veterinary surgeon rasps the teeth, working hard and frequently washing the residue away by dipping the rasp into clean water. Sometimes an assistant holds the donkey's tongue safely out of the way at one side of his mouth while the vet works on the other side. It gives the donkey no pain, and ours have never objected in any way, although it may look uncomfortable. It can make a great difference to the nourishment your donkey gets from the food you supply.

16 Feet

Donkeys, from smallest foal to aged animal, have attractive feet, if they are well kept. Once again we have to remember the donkey's origins: those hot stony deserts. Then think of the lush green fields and soft straw our donkeys walk on. A donkey's hoof, as with all equines, is composed of material similar to our fingernails, and like our nails it keeps growing all through their lives. If they are living wild in the desert, roaming over vast territories and cantering across stony land, their feet are kept worn down. A donkey who is regularly ridden or driven on hard roads will wear his hooves also, but too much, and, like a horse, a donkey working on the roads needs to be shod.

A pet donkey who only carries shopping from the village shop or gives a small child a ride along a country road and spends the rest of his time on grass or straw will need to have his hooves trimmed regularly. As a donkey's foot grows it elongates at the front, forcing the donkey down on his heels; then it starts to turn up in front and curl under at one or both sides until it is almost impossible for the poor animal to walk at all. To let a donkey's feet get to this condition is cruel, because not only is he unable to walk, but his legs can be strained and be permanently damaged.

This is why I said at the beginning of the book do not have a donkey if you are unable to get a farrier. Farriers are enormously

If your donkey is restless when having his feet cleaned try giving him a small bowl of food.

skilled craftsmen. They are strong, too, and with a flick of their wrists can cut the hard hoof of a donkey or horse into shape. They have served a long apprenticeship and must pass examinations before they are allowed to practise their skilled work.

Farriers will tell you that donkeys' feet vary in some points from horses' and need to be trimmed in a different way. A horse's hoof is much more brittle and will probably chip off before it gets to the uncomfortable stage: one seldom sees a horse or pony, even an unshod mare in a field or on a common, with really bad feet, but twenty years ago it was a familiar sight here and in Ireland to see donkeys with turned-up toes. We must thank the Donkey Breed Society for this improvement as ever since its inception it has put out information and propaganda about the care of donkeys' feet. It is difficult to say exactly how often you will need to get a farrier to attend to your pet's feet. Some hooves grow much more quickly than others, but I would think the average donkey would need his feet trimmed every eight weeks.

The donkey's hoof consists of a horny wall which protects the sole and is attached to it by a thin layer of lighter horn called the white line. At the back is the frog, a triangular piece of more elastic horn which takes the pressure from the delicate parts of the inside of the foot. Your farrier will cut or clip back the horny wall of the foot and carefully hollow out the sole so that your donkey walks on the outer edge — the horn wall — of his foot. If the sole grows proud of the wall of the hoof, so that the donkey is walking on it, it not only makes him rock unevenly, but should he walk on a stone the sole can get bruised, which will make him lame. The frog at the back of a horse's foot will need to be trimmed with the rest of his foot, but donkeys have small frogs and they seldom need attention. When you are cleaning out his foot, do not prod the soles too harshly with a sharp metal pick, especially round the frog.

Lameness in donkeys is nine times out of ten due to their feet. First you must find out which foot is affected and, unless it is so painful he stands on three legs, this can be surprisingly difficult. If it is one of his front feet a lame donkey when he is walking or trotting will drop his head as the good foreleg hits the ground. If it is a hind foot, you can see when you stand behind him that he does not lift the bad leg so much, and the point of the hock of the good leg is lifted higher.

First clean out his hoof gently but thoroughly and make sure he has not got a stone wedged against his sole, a nail or even a thorn piercing his foot between the sole and the wall. A ball of hard mud or snow can make him lame. If you find the cause of the trouble and remove it, either by gently prising it out or with tweezers, unless it has penetrated his foot through the hoof, no more action needs to be taken. If his foot has been penetrated by a long nail or anything else that draws blood, his foot should be stood in warm salted water for a few minutes and washed as clean as possible. When it bleeds the flow of blood helps to wash away infection so do not be in a hurry to staunch it. You may need to bandage his foot and even put a little boot on: a really thick plastic bag, or two bags, over his foot can keep him clean for a night if he is confined to his stable, but be careful not to tie the top of the bags too tightly round his leg or you will stop his circulation.

If the object needs to be cut out of his sole you must get a vet. I am presuming that your donkey is up to date with his anti-tetanus injections; if he is not and he gets any wound in his foot you must get in touch with your vet at once and have him immunized.

Should a donkey's hoof become infected, swelling, which is one of the characteristic symbols of inflammation, is impossible because the sensitive parts of his foot are enclosed in the rigid box of his hoof, and consequently he will suffer great pain. The infection is driven upwards to his coronet and can go up his leg and all through his body. So if his foot is causing him pain even when he is not walking on it, get your vet in good time so that he can treat the foot and give antibiotics to prevent the poison spreading.

Seedy toe is the most common cause of trouble found in donkeys' feet. Animals from Ireland frequently suffered from seedy toe in their neglected feet. Once it has taken hold you cannot get rid of it until that part of the hoof has grown down and been pared away. It is due to an infection in the white line between the wall and the sole of the hoof and causes a small black hole which gradually spreads upwards and sideways. Although not caused by wet it is certainly exacerbated by it and if your donkey has a tendency to seedy toe it will help if you can keep him shut in at night.

If caught in time seedy toe can easily be eliminated, and it should never be allowed to take such a hold that your farrier is unable to cut it away each time your donkey's feet are trimmed. If the hole is deeper than he is able to trim away he will have to clean out the hole thoroughly, cutting away as much as he can, and dress the hole with Terramycin or Aureomycin. We had some donkeys from Ireland who arrived with such enormous patches of seedy toe that the farrier used to plug the hole with Stockholm tar and cotton wool once they were cleaned out, which he did so skilfully it would

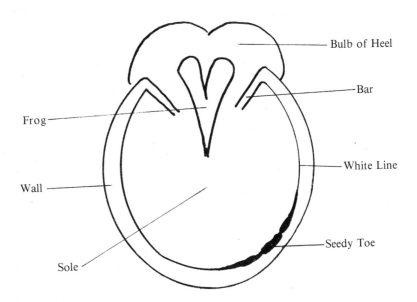

A donkey's hoof showing seedy toe. Seedy toe develops in the white line and extends upwards. It is naturally filled with crumbly horn, but soon picks up dirt and small stones and often infection. It usually is found near the front of the foot.

still be in place at his next visit. Eventually, with frequent trimming and the farrier's care, it grew out.

Laminitis is another much dreaded foot problem and is more serious because once a donkey has suffered from laminitis it is liable to recur. It normally attacks at least two feet, either the two front or the two back, at the same time and is distressingly painful.

The cause is not fully known but, curiously, eating too much rich food, particularly when combined with too little exercise, can be a factor, especially if the donkey is overweight and therefore putting extra strain on his feet. If his hooves are not regularly trimmed it also appears to make him more vulnerable. It is fairly easy to diagnose: he will spend much of his time lying down and will be reluctant to move. If his back feet are affected he will place them forward, well beneath his belly, so that he stands on his heels. If it is his front feet he will keep them forward so that he stands on his front heels. Although the hooves of a horse or pony always feel hot when it is suffering from laminitis this is not noticeable with a donkey. You will have to call your vet who will be able to relieve the pain, and will put him on a diet and tell you how to manage him. He will need a lot of care and sympathy.

You should be able to avoid laminitis in the first place by not overfeeding, rationing your donkey's intake of spring grass, keeping his feet well trimmed and making sure that he has adequate regular exercise. It has been found that pasture which has been newly treated with nitrogen is particularly dangerous, and so is a field growing a lot of clover.

Cracks Hooves can suffer from cracks, starting either at the coronet and running downwards or from the base upwards, and they can also get chipped and broken. If your donkey's feet are trimmed regularly your farrier will deal with these problems.

17 *Parasites*

All donkeys have parasites. So for that matter do horses, dogs, cats and budgerigars. Even parasites frequently have parasites. A parasite is an animal living in or on another animal, and although it is impossible to eliminate them entirely they must be kept down to an acceptable level.

Intestinal worms A great variety of worms infest donkeys. There are many varieties of red worms (strongyles) and these and white worms *(parascaris equorum)* are the most important intestinal worms affecting equines. All worms have slightly different life cycles, but fortunately they can all be controlled in the same way. If you are interested in the varied and fascinating life cycles of parasites you should read about them in a veterinary dictionary. Briefly, the eggs of the worms are passed onto the pasture in the dung of the donkey and are picked up again, either as eggs or as the hatched larvae, when he is grazing. They breed inside the donkey, migrate through the intestinal wall and then through various abdominal tissues. Some species spend part of their life in the animal's blood vessels, causing obstructions, others spend time in the lungs or liver and migrate through the body, causing damage to many of the organs before becoming adult and returning to the intestines to lay more eggs which are passed out of the donkey onto the grass. The cycle starts again when the donkey, horse or pony picks them up when eating. Cattle and sheep have their own varieties of worms and can pick up those from equines without being harmed, and vice versa.

While it is impossible to rid a donkey completely of intestinal worms, they can be kept to a minimum if they are killed inside the donkey by the use of anthelmintics and if the pasture is managed so that the donkey reinfests himself as little as possible.

An expert can recognize a wormy donkey on sight. He is usually thin, with hollows in front of his hips, but with a large stomach. His hair is rough and dull and he is often listless and irritable. He may eat everything ravenously but as the infestation increases he will probably have a depressed appetite. His dung might be soft and runny. Worms make a donkey uncomfortable and consequently naughty. A donkey who is restless in his stable, bites or kicks out at you or other donkeys, refuses to be led and is generally short-tempered is often wormy and when he is back to good health you would be surprised how sweet natured he really is.

Youngstock are more often affected than older donkeys and can be seriously damaged and it is most important to see that they are kept as free from worms as possible.

The burden of larvae in a paddock can be greatly reduced by proper management. Vast numbers of eggs are distributed on the pasture and the young worms from these can live for long periods in damp shady places. The numbers are reduced by the lapse of time, by frost and by dry, arid conditions. Unfortunately in this country they are often kept alive by the heavy dews at night. This is why I suggested that your donkey's field should be divided into two or even three paddocks: while he is grazing one the others can have a rest, each paddock being used for three or four weeks only. If it is possible for the resting paddocks to have sheep or cattle on them they will clean up the donkey's worms without being affected themselves. Should you have plenty of land you could make hay in one field.

Foals and youngstock can be seriously damaged by parasites picked up in their paddocks and must be treated regularly and more often than adult donkeys. A group of foals romping together including Marius, Simon, Joseph, Elizabeth Ann, Cordelia, Desdemona and Sarah Jane.

Keeping the pasture short by topping it when the donkey is moved out will improve the damp patches of longer grass where the worms thrive. Best of all pick up the donkey's droppings every night; this really is effective, and is not too arduous if it is done at once before it is walked into the grass or rained on.

Giving anthelmintics used to be one of the most difficult jobs in looking after a donkey. Donkeys are much too clever to eat food laced with worming powder, and drenching a donkey is a task to be avoided — more of the drench invariably goes onto the handler than down the animal's throat, and one is terrified of pouring it into his lungs and drowning him. Science has come to our aid and now it is no longer dangerous for him or difficult for us. The anthelmintic is bought in a syringe in the form of paste and all we have to do is to squirt it into the back of the donkey's mouth. He will make faces for a few minutes, and when you are certain he has swallowed it all you can give him a biscuit to take the taste away — but wait until his mouth is empty or he will smear the paste onto the biscuit and spit the whole thing out.

The syringe containing the anthelmintic is marked in doses and if a donkey is not mentioned in the instructions give him half the dose recommended for a pony. The drugs are so safe that even if you gave him twice the correct dose it would not harm him.

Lungworm We hear a great deal about lungworm *(dictyocaulus)* because the owners of horses and ponies accuse donkeys of infesting their animals. If a horse or pony is even slightly infested it will probably cough and be treated, but donkeys seldom cough unless the infestation is severe (although their lungs may be damaged), so it is wise to treat them twice a year with one of the preparations specially recommended, such as Dicaracide or Nilverm, or with the recommended dose of Thiabendazole.

Lungworm live most of their lives in the bronchial tubes of an equine's lungs, where they lay their eggs. These eggs are coughed up and swallowed and then evacuated in dung onto the pasture. There they eventually become infective larvae and are swallowed by the animal and carried to the intestines where they penetrate the intestinal wall and migrate through the bloodstream to the lungs.

On the pasture the larvae are killed by drought but can withstand fairly low temperatures. Presumably donkeys suffer little from any kind of parasitic worms in their natural habitat where they range daily over large areas of arid land. Here, where they are kept in such different conditions, we need to protect them by keeping the pastures as clean as possible and killing all we can inside the donkey.

It is possible to have the faeces of the donkey examined by a vet who can count the various parasites present in the dung and advise you about dosing your donkey, but unless you think you might have a special problem it is sufficient to dose him every three months: if you feel he is in poor condition you should seek your vet's advice anyway.

Bot and warble fly Warble flies rarely attack a donkey with success; I have never seen one which has been affected. Bot flies lay their eggs in the summer on the hairs, usually of the legs. When the donkey licks them off and swallows them they complete their cycle inside his body attached to the wall of his stomach where they interfere with his digestion and can cause stomach ulcers. By far the best cure is prevention. Give him a dark shelter from the flies in the summer and if any eggs are seen on his coat during his daily grooming either pull or cut them off— you cannot brush them off. The eggs are tiny and yellow but quite visible. Warble fly eggs are laid on the hair in the same way and have to be cut off. In case you miss any bot fly eggs it is advisable to dose your donkey in the autumn with a worming treatment that contains dichlorvos.

A parasite can become resistant to any anthelmintic which is used repeatedly so it is wise to change from one drug to another during the year. As the autumn is the only time possible to eradicate bot fly the following is a good routine:

March: A bendazole-based paste
June: Haloxon
August: A bendazole-based paste
October: Dichlorvos, which will eliminate bots

Dose at the rate suggested for donkeys or at half the rate for ponies.

Lice Some donkeys seem much more prone to lice than others, but even the most louse-free animal should be protected in the spring and autumn.

There are three kinds of lice that attack donkeys, but none of these can live on a human or any non-equine animal, so you need not worry about them biting you. Two of these lice bite and one sucks, but as they are all treated the same way there is no need to know which type or types your donkey suffers from. Usually the first symptom is the donkey rubbing himself, often at the beginning of spring, followed by bare patches on his skin. The hair comes off in tufts leaving a perfectly clean skin, with no scabs or sore places, although he may rub himself sore later. If the hair comes off leaving scabs, sores or running mucus it is not lice and you must have him examined by a vet.

If your donkey is showing symptoms of lice treat him at once with a farmyard louse powder or one sold for equines, and rub it in generously, parting his hair down his spine and concentrating on the tops of his front legs and around the bald patches. It is necessary to use plenty of powder and repeat the treatment every two weeks for about two months as the eggs, called nits, are not killed. Although it is difficult to see the lice you can often see the nits, especially on a dark-haired donkey; they are tiny, slightly long-shaped, cream-coloured eggs, and they cling to the hair, especially round the bald patches.

If possible powder the donkey out of doors on a still day; in the stable you both breathe the powder and he might get some in his eyes. In severe cases the donkey can be shampooed with a special preparation, or even clipped out, but neither of these remedies is advised except in a hot summer; powder and determination will clear up the trouble in time.

Mange is caused by mites, too small to see, which produce intense irritation and the hair falls out leaving scabby, sore patches sometimes oozing a sticky mucus. You must get your vet as it is a serious condition and some kinds of mange must be notified to the Ministry of Agriculture. Your vet will take a scraping of the skin and send it to a laboratory to have the type of mange identified. Meantime you must isolate your donkey for it is infectious to other animals.

Fortunately mange is unusual in donkeys and normally only occurs in animals that are dirty and neglected.

18 Troubles from Ear to Tail and how to avoid them

EARS

Bog itch used to be common in donkeys arriving from Ireland. Usually the ears are affected first, then the top of the head and neck, the nose and sometimes the lower part of the legs. It is really just bad chapping; a rough, scabby condition caused by constant subjection to rain, and it is not infectious. The hair gets matted and falls off and the skin becomes encrusted with little scabs and spots. In severe cases the skin is hot and painful when touched. Foals and young donkeys are more affected than adults, presumably because their hair soaks up the rain more.

It is easy to avoid: the donkey should never have been kept out in the rain without shelter. To cure it rub on soothing and waterproof ointment such as zinc and castor oil or even coat the ears with petroleum jelly, and make sure he is shut inside when it is raining.

If his skin becomes infected through rubbing, or it is so bad it is making him miserable, you will need to get your vet.

Canker is a general term used for almost any infection inside the ear. Fortunately donkeys seldom have ear trouble although some produce so much soft wax it hangs on the fluff of their ears and looks unattractive. This just needs teasing off the hair, and the immediate inside of the ear should be cleaned out gently with a paper handkerchief. Never probe inside your donkey's ears yourself, and if they appear scabby or raw inside, or have any discharge other than wax, you must call your vet.

EYES

Flies are the commonest cause of sore eyes in donkeys. They

(Above) *Donkeys suffering from flies and* (opposite) *the veil to protect them*

drink the moisture at the corners of the eyes, causing them to water
more freely, and eventually they make a hole in the skin, which
encourages more flies. As the donkey tries to rub them off on his
legs he makes matters worse by rubbing his face raw. If you put
ointment on the sore you can be sure he will rub it into his eyes, so
if these sores have been neglected and are causing him discomfort
you will need to get your vet to give you a special ointment which is
safe to use near his eyes.

It is easy to prevent this trouble from flies by giving him a dark
shelter he can go into during the day and using an insect repellant
that has been specially made for animals around his ears and

forehead. The anti-fly ear tags made for cattle are effective but the problem is how to attach them to your donkey as you are unlikely to want to tag his ear; they can be attached to a headcollar, or to a belt round the donkey's neck, but normally donkeys do not wear either.

The most effective way of keeping his eyes free from flies is to make him a fly veil. This is a piece of curtain net with a tape at top and bottom; the veiling may be gathered or tucked into the tape but this is not necessary. The top tape ties round the back of his ears and the bottom tape ties under his chin. He can see through the net and it keeps him completely free from flies round his eyes. It means

a little extra work: first to make the veil and then to repair it when he catches it on a twig. It will also need to be washed now and again, using a mild soap rather than a detergent. There is no doubt donkeys like wearing a veil; if any of ours loses or tears theirs on a sultry day he soon comes to the fence and shouts for another.

Stings and wounds Donkeys can get stung on or near their eyes when they disturb a bee or wasp in the grass or can be wounded with a sharp piece of stick or stalk when grazing. If his eye looks sore and keeps watering call your vet who can give you an opthalmic antibiotic to put in his eye. It is always dangerous to neglect any eye trouble.

Blocked tear duct Donkeys, like other animals and ourselves,

A donkey with a blocked tear duct. Having a constantly running eye not only attracts flies but can make the skin sore if neglected.

produce a clear liquid to keep their eyes washed and lubricated. This is drained away through a tube which runs from the inner corner of the eye into the nostril. If this tube gets blocked the tears cannot get away and overflow down his face. Unless the duct has been damaged by an injury the trouble is caused by an infection and your vet will treat it.

HEAD

Stroke It is possible for a donkey to have a stroke. You will know at once that something is wrong as he will be in pain, will be confused, and possibly will walk round and round in small circles. He is likely to be in considerable pain so send for your vet at once and while you are waiting for him to arrive stay with your donkey to reassure him, keep him warm with a blanket over his back, and if possible keep him in the dark.

We had a little mare who suffered from a stroke and eventually made what appeared to be a complete recovery thanks to the skill of our vet, although it took some months, so do not give up hope.

NOSE AND THROAT

Running nose A running nose can be the first visible sign of various ailments and we must hope it is nothing more serious than a slight cold. To be on the safe side isolate your donkey from other equines and keep him warm but make sure the ventilation is good. It is better to put him in a stable with the top of the door open and wearing a blanket than to keep him in a stuffy atmosphere. If the weather is good he can stay outside during the day. Try to keep his nose clean: it may just need to be wiped with a paper handkerchief or it may discharge mucus which should be washed away with warm salty water.

If he is listless or off his food, if he seems to be breathing more quickly than usual, or is making a sound when he breathes, you must get your vet at once. If you wait for a day or two to see if he gets better his ailment will be more difficult to treat.

Coughing can be a symptom of various troubles. Horse owners usually first think of lungworm but many donkeys who are quite badly infected never cough at all. Lungworm is discussed on page 53.

If a donkey rolls in a dust patch or gets a hayseed caught in his throat he may cough a couple of times to clear his throat and invariably follows up with a sneeze, but if he coughs persistently he needs attention, as it can indicate a virus infection or even pneumonia and it is best to get your vet to investigate promptly.

Influenza is caused by a virus infection and it seems to affect donkeys more seriously than horses. The symptoms are a running nose and sometimes running eyes as well, with a cough and general malaise — he will have a temperature. Keep him warm, with plenty of fresh air, away from other equines, and send for your vet.

It is wise to have your donkey vaccinated against equine influenza. The first injection is followed by another in two month's time and an annual booster is needed every year; it can be given in the same injection as his anti-tetanus vaccine. If you contemplate taking your donkey to a show you may be required to produce his certificate of immunization against equine influenza.

Sinusitus is due to infection in the hollow bones of the face, usually starting in the nose or throat, but sometimes in the teeth. It can be recognized by a persistant discharge of mucus from, generally, only one nostril. Your vet will try to clear it with antibiotics, but sometimes an abscess has to be drained by making openings in the bones of the face so that the pus can escape. When the abscess is cured, the wounds heal quickly. If the infection is caused by a tooth the removal of the tooth will usually allow the pus to drain. The only donkey I have known who suffered from sinus trouble was in very poor condition, and with treatment from the vet the condition disappeared once she was in better health.

Sore throat Donkeys can get sore throats from an external irritation such as eating something prickly — I knew a donkey who had a passion for sweet chestnuts with unfortunate results — but it is more often an infection so contact your veterinary surgeon.

Strangles When we first kept donkeys strangles was a fairly common complaint. It is extremely infectious, but only to equines, and can be picked up in a dealer's yard, a transport box or anywhere a number of horses and donkeys have been kept together. It has an incubation period of eight days, so, although it is much less common now, if you are introducing a new donkey to your equines and he has been travelling with other donkeys or horses, or if you bought him at a market, you should keep him on his own for just over a week.

The symptoms start like an ordinary cold but he soon develops very swollen glands under his jaw and around his throat. Abscesses form which eventually burst with a discharge of highly infectious pus. Once again if he appears to have anything more than a very slight cold keep him away from his equine friends and send for your vet.

Teeth are discussed on page 81.

CHEST

Pneumonia Donkeys, especially young donkeys, are susceptible to pneumonia so we need to be particularly careful not to neglect a cold or chill, all the more because it damages an animal's lungs permanently. Make sure your donkey has a dry, draught-proof stable or shed available at all times with warm bedding on the floor and plenty of ventilation above donkey level. If he is coughing or has a running nose and you can hear any signs of wheezing, if he is breathing quickly or seems listless, send for your vet and tell him what is the matter. The sooner pneumonia is treated the better; fortunately, if caught in time, it reacts successfully to antibiotics. Your vet will give you instructions about nursing and it may be months, rather than weeks, before he has recovered.

STOMACH

Colic is the name given to anything that causes pain in a donkey's stomach and bowels and as a donkey is incapable of being sick he is unable to get rid of the substance which is causing the pain. Partially digested food can ferment and cause gases which distend the stomach and intestines painfully and the nerves, if irritated, can cause gripping spasms of the muscles.

The poor donkey will make it quite plain to you that he is in pain. He will lie down and roll, stand up again and look round at, or even bite at his stomach. He may be calm for a few minutes when the pain subsides but will drop down and start to roll again. All you can do is to send urgently for your vet, telling him what is

the matter, and while you are waiting for him to arrive try to keep
your donkey warm with a rug or old blanket, as he will probably
already be in a state of shock, and as calm as possible to prevent
him injuring himself. Stay with him and try to comfort and
reassure him. We used to be told that an animal should be walked
about and prevented from rolling but now it is thought that rolling
cannot harm him — any harm has already been done and causes
him to roll. However you might be able to keep him under better
control if he will walk about.

There are drenches for colic which often contain ether and can
ease the pain, but never dose your donkey with one of these unless
it has been supplied by your vet and you have his permission to use
it, otherwise it might prevent him giving other treatment. If you
have permission to give a colic medicine dilute it as instructed with
warm water and pour it, a little at a time, into your donkey's
mouth, rubbing his throat so that he has to swallow it. A plastic
bottle, such as lemonade is supplied in, is a safe dispenser as he is
probably agitated and could break a glass bottle.

Your vet will try to find out the cause and type of the colic. It
might be a simple colic due to gas in the bowel or it could be more
complicated; you can only leave it to the skill of your vet who will
certainly be able to relieve the pain and reduce the spasms.

As colic is such an unpleasant experience for your donkey, and
for you too, it is worth going to trouble to avoid it. One of the
causes is a bad infestation of worms, but your donkey will be
protected against this. Unsuitable food, or even too rapid a change
from one type of food to another can cause indigestion; the most
dangerous foods are those which swell inside him such as unsoaked
beet pulp, hen food, pig food or wheat. If he opens his food bin
and grossly overeats, it could cause colic. Mouldy hay or straw or
dirty feeding bowls are dangerous.

Toxic weeds or trees can poison him and if the grass is sparse he
is more likely to try unusual herbage, so if you are putting him out
onto a bare paddock make sure he has a full stomach before he
goes and a net of hay or straw to eat if he gets hungry. You must
also do this before putting him out into the snow or to eat grass
covered in frost and if you are letting him eat lush spring grass the
same applies: he should go out with his appetite already satisfied
and only be left out for a few hours at a time.

Lawn mowings can ferment and he can eat too many too quickly because they need no chewing. Which leads to teeth: if he is not chewing his food properly he is putting a burden on his digestion, so do not neglect to have his teeth inspected regularly.

Lastly, make sure there are no hazards such as pieces of plastic or wire in his paddock which he could pick up while he is grazing and which could stick in his stomach or intestines.

Mastitis is infection of the udder and the most usual times for a donkey to suffer are when a foal is being weaned, especially if it is weaned too early, or while she is feeding a foal, but it is possible for a mare to be infected when she is neither in foal nor suckling.

The start of mastitis. The left side of the mare's udder is larger and the teat more swollen than the right side.

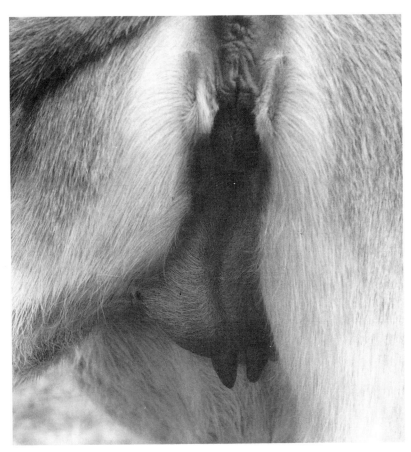

The udder is swollen, feels hot and hard and is extremely painful, especially when touched, making her walk stiffly. Frequently the infection only attacks one side, or attacks one side before the other, making the udder lopsided. The infection spreads to her body if it is not treated, and can cause death if gangrene sets in. Ask your vet to come as soon as possible as mastitis responds well to antibiotics if treated early enough. If you ever notice that your mare has a pronounced lopsided udder call your vet at once.

Twisted gut means that the intestines have folded themselves in such a way as to be completely blocked. It is almost impossible to distinguish this from other colic in time to operate so it is nearly always fatal. The symptoms are the same as for any other form of colic so your vet will be there to relieve the pain.

LEGS

Lameness We have already discussed a donkey being lame due to his feet in Chapter 16 and suggested that this is where the trouble usually lies; it is possible however that he might have strained or sprained a leg or that he could be suffering from a bruise. If he seems to be in severe pain, or is refusing to walk on one leg, you must get your vet to examine him, but if he only has a small unevenness of gait and you have examined his feet as suggested, you could watch him carefully for a day or two before you seek assistance. He should not be worked in any way of course but neither must you allow him to stand perfectly still without exercise. If his lameness gets worse, if he is reluctant to move, if he is miserable or loses his appetite you must get the vet, but otherwise it is safe to wait and see if time will effect a cure.

Mud fever occurs when mud is allowed to cake round a donkey's hoof, especially his heels and coronet, which pulls away the hair causing local infection and sores. I have seen a donkey with the mud caked so solidly she was unable to bend her ankles and was lame on all legs. You must get the mud off so gently it does not pull on the hair at all. It is best to put each foot in turn into a bucket of tepid water and wash the mud away a little at a time as it softens. In the case of the poor donkey who was unable to walk it took a couple of days to remove all the mud but was completely

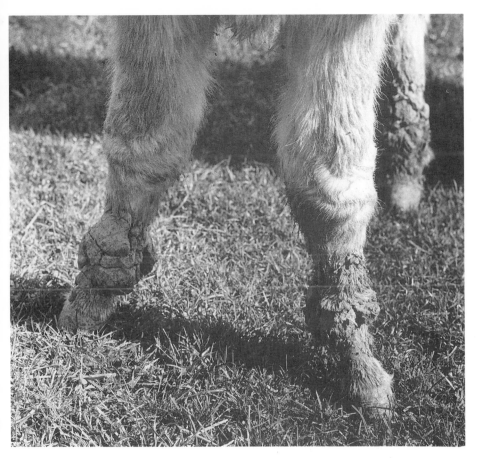

Mud is badly caked round the donkey's ankles. You can see the hair has come away on the near fore-leg.

successful, leaving her with no infection or soreness. If bare flesh is exposed as the mud comes away, dry it carefully and treat it with a soothing ointment such as zinc and castor oil, or, if it is raw, with an antibiotic spray. Should the donkey be badly infected round the heels and coronet you will have to send for your vet.

BACK END

Bot flies The larvae of the bot can cause irritation round the donkey's anus and you may see him rubbing his backside on a rail or tree (see page 93).

Sore anus The anus ring through which the dung is evacuated can become sore and split. This happens more often in a young or elderly donkey who is not provided with enough shelter from the rain which runs under his tail and causes chapping. If it hurts a donkey to dung he may hold it back and become constipated. Look under his tail when you groom him and if it looks dry or cracked gently rub in some zinc and castor oil ointment. If you find he is not passing faeces, or only seldom (a donkey normally dungs about every two hours) you must contact your vet.

Constipation Unless a donkey is holding back from dunging for some reason, constipation is unusual — think of all the fibre they consume every day! The best cure for slight constipation is plenty of water to drink — he might be more tempted if it is slightly warm — and a dose of liquid paraffin. For an average size donkey mix half a pint of liquid paraffin with an equal quantity of warm water and, holding up his head, pour it into his mouth a little at a time, rubbing and tapping his throat to encourage him to swallow. If there is no improvement you must send for your vet as it is important to discover the cause of the complaint as well as to cure it. If a foal is constipated you must get your vet at once.

Scouring (diarrhoea) can be caused by eating unsuitable food, such as too much wet grass, or poison of some kind; by intestinal worms; by an infection of the intestines or by fright or fear.

If a donkey is very loose, that is, when the dung is liquid and is squirting out, and this continues for more than two hours, you must send for your veterinary surgeon, as the donkey might get dehydrated; it is especially dangerous for foals or youngstock and you need to get help as soon as possible.

However if the dung is of the consistency of cow dung, keep him in his stable with only hay or straw to eat, but with his usual bucket of water, and if he does not improve in twenty-four hours ask your vet to call.

Prolapse A prolapse is when the inside of the anus, or the vagina if it is a mare or filly, slips so that it appears on the outside. Should this occur keep the part as clean as possible, but do not wash with anything other than salt and water, and send for your vet. It is invariably symptomatic of poor condition and most often occurs in youngstock which have not been well cared-for.

TAIL

A donkey's tail is usually free from trouble except that, like his ears at the other end, the skin round the top of his tail and on the insides of his back legs is one of the places he can suffer from bog itch. Ponies have a bunch of hair at the top of their tails which protects them from the wet, but rain runs down beside and under the tail of a donkey, and can cause chapping and chilling. Treat it with a waterproof, soothing ointment such as zinc and castor oil. It is an indication that he is not being given adequate shelter.

It takes a long time for the hair on a donkey's tail to grow again if he loses it through some mishap. I have known one donkey to have the hair of his tail nibbled away by a goat and another who stood too near to a bonfire. But these things don't happen often.

19 General Troubles

Allergies Donkeys can be allergic to any of the usual irritants such as dusty hay, mouldy straw, pollens, foods, insects bites, etc. I knew a donkey who was allergic to hoof parings; apparently not her own, but when she was held beside a nervous friend who was having her feet trimmed she reacted immediately.

An allergy can take the form of a loss of hair, spots or rashes on the skin, or a running nose and eyes; or a donkey can react quickly to an irritant which can make his face and throat, and usually his rectum, swell so severely that he has difficulty in breathing, his eyes close and his lips and nostrils become greatly swollen. If this happens you must send for your vet at once, telling him what has happened. In the meantime take the animal away from anything you think might have brought on the condition: if he is in a field take him into a stable; if he is inside take him out into the air. His appearance is frightening, and it can be serious, but he will probably respond quickly to an anti-histamine injection which the vet will give him.

Bumps and lumps Donkeys can grow various bumps and lumps, sometimes on the skin, such as warts, and sometimes under the skin showing only as a swelling.

If he has a small wart on his skin which is not growing quickly, and it is not in a position where it gets rubbed or causes him any bother, there is no panic, but show it to your vet the next time he comes to innoculate your donkey.

A rash of spots occurring in the summer, possibly down his chest and the top of his legs, is probably due to insect bites or even nettle stings; anoint him with benzyl benzoate every third day until it disappears.

Any wart or lump on or under the skin which grows rapidly or causes discomfort should be examined by your vet.

Ringworm is the only infection that donkeys can pass on to other non-equine animals and to humans, so although in itself it is not serious for the donkey it is important it should be diagnosed and treated at once. It is contagious rather than infectious as it is caused by a fungus, but the spores can be airborne and cling to posts, the interior of horse boxes, old tack, etc., for months.

The first time I saw ringworm on a donkey I failed to recognize it because the only form of ringworm I knew was on cattle, which makes a red circle that gradually expands as the inside of the ring heals. We had a little filly, who came from Ireland and was ill, living in our kitchen. After a few weeks I developed an obvious infection on my wrist, showing all the usual symptoms, and I rushed to my doctor showing him my arm and bewailing the fact that I would give ringworm to the donkeys. 'Most unlikely,' he said, 'After all, it is not as if they were living with you in the house.'

A check with our vet soon confirmed that Columbine had ringworm too, but on a donkey it starts as a little round bald patch about the size of a new penny, frequently on the face or shoulder. As it gets bigger the skin becomes rough and scabby and the hair around it is often matted, but it never makes the usual circle. It is easily cured: your vet can prescribe a drug which is taken by mouth, or it can be treated with one of the aerosol sprays sold for the purpose, but it is usually a symptom of poor condition generally, and your vet may give the donkey a course of vitamins as well as curing the infection.

He will have to be kept away from all other animals, and you must be scrupulously careful with his grooming kit.

My ringworm cleared up as quickly as Columbine's with the help of an ointment from my doctor.

Sweet itch can be distressing and you have to spend time and take some trouble to keep it under control. It appears in spring as a series of lumps, like insect bites, generally down the mane and along the back to the root of the tail, but sometimes more widely spread onto the chest, the top of the legs and the stomach. These bites erupt and weep and can cause the donkey such irritation that he will rub himself raw. A donkey suffering from neglected sweet itch is a pathetic sight, most of his hair rubbed off and unable to stop rubbing and biting himself.

Only recently it has been discovered that the cause of this condition is a small midge, and that these midges only bite for a few hours before and after sunset. It is therefore possible to avoid them by stabling your donkey in a dark box in the late afternoon, with a frequently renewed insecticide strip hung well out of reach over his head. We have found that covering the affected parts of the donkey with benzyl benzoate every fourth day can keep him clear from bites, but we have also found that the area bitten by the midges can extend as they seek untreated skin, and I have known a donkey to have badly bitten legs when her body was protected. The benzyl benzoate needs to be well rubbed into her skin and this takes time.

Donkeys that are badly affected in one part of the country can be free from sweet itch in another county.

If sweet itch gets out of hand and he is rubbing himself raw you will have to ask your vet for help.

Tetanus, commonly known as lockjaw, is caused by a bacillus that lives in the soil and in animal manure. It becomes active once it enters the animal through a scratch or wound and the incubation period can vary from a week to a few months. Sometimes no wound can be found and in these cases the infection may have entered through the bowel, where the tetanus germs are always present in large numbers, but are harmless unless there is damage caused by worms or some other irritant. The donkey nearly always dies in great pain and it is a most distressing disease to witness.

Fortunately the hazard of tetanus can easily be avoided by having your donkey immunized and it is imperative that you do so. The donkey is vaccinated with tetanus toxoid, which creates anti-bodies ready to deal with the infection, followed by a booster one month later and another booster in twelve months. For the rest of his life he will need a booster every second year. Your vet will advise you about immunizing in-foal mares and young foals.

It is said that no one who has witnessed a death from tetanus would ever leave an animal unprotected.

Not only your donkey, but you, too, should be immunized.

Wounds and scratches If a wound is deep, bleeding excessively or if it needs a stitch to hold the flesh together, you must get in touch with your vet at once. Most wounds are best left alone, so that the blood can clot, until they have skilled attention, but if the bleeding is excessive you should cover the wound with a clean cloth or cotton wool and apply pressure.

Wounds that puncture deeply, like those caused by a hayfork, are exceptionally dangerous so do not think they are insignificant because the area of broken skin is small.

Scratches, scrapes and flesh wounds should be cleaned with salt water and sprayed with antibiotic. During the summer an anti-fly repellant such as Negasunt is useful.

If your donkey has not been immunized against tetanus you must send for your vet immediately for any wound.

General hints Always send for your veterinary surgeon as soon as you suspect illness. Not only will it be less expensive in the end, but you will give him every opportunity to effect a quick and complete cure. Send for him at once if your donkey is off his food for more than twenty-four hours, if he seems to be in pain or to be confused, if his breathing is rapid or harsh or if he seems distressed in any way.

While you are waiting for your vet keep him warm, but not stuffy — a warm rug and an infra-red lamp with the door open is better than having him shut in a stable with an airless atmosphere. If you have no special donkey rug use an old blanket or a big bath towel. Natural materials are warmer and more absorbent than man-made ones. If you suspect he has a temperature make sure he is not in a draught. Stuff any cracks or holes in his stable with straw and put a bale of straw inside the bottom of the door, but leave the top of the door open unless it is blowing icy wind or rain from that direction. Keep him away from other equines in case he is infectious or contagious.

Do not use any antiseptic or disinfectant on your donkey except on your vet's instructions. Use them on your own hands and on equipment, but salt water is best for cleaning scrapes or sores and for washing mucus from his eyes or nose — a dessertspoon of salt to a pint of water.

If you have to give your donkey medicine, hold up his head and pour a little at a time into his mouth from a plastic bottle, rubbing and tapping his throat to make him swallow, and allowing him to lower his head frequently. It can be difficult, and it is best to take it slowly so that you do not frighten him or make him choke.

Do follow your vet's instructions implicitly. Give the donkey the correct doses of medicine for the number of days you have been told, and do not think that because your animal seems better you can stop the treatment.

You will want to keep a small 'medicine cupboard' for your donkey. He will not need much: worming paste and louse powder are necessities and so is an animal fly repellant. You will also need an antibiotic, obtainable from your vet, for slight wounds and sores, a soothing ointment such as zinc and castor oil, benzyl benzoate for insect bites and bumps, salt to put in the water for cleaning scrapes or dirty noses. Cotton wool is useful but needs to be kept clean, and if you keep a pair of blunt-ended scissors with the other remedies it will save you hunting for one in an emergency. Only keep a colic medicine if supplied by your vet.

This seems a long list of troubles and illnesses, but I assure you a well cared-for donkey is a healthy animal and you are most unlikely to need to refer to this chapter again. Donkeys are much less prone to accidents than horses or ponies — dare I say because they are more intelligent? — and provided you remember that donkeys come from a hot dry country and shelter and feed your donkey accordingly, he will have a long troublefree life and reward you for the time and energy you use to keep him in perfect condition.

20 *The Pros and Cons of Having a Foal*

Perhaps you are considering letting your donkey mare have a foal, or perhaps you are going to buy a donkey and you think it would be pleasant to get a mare already in foal.

The pleasures of having a donkey foal are so obvious they hardly need enumerating. I am certain there is no other young animal with the appeal of a baby donkey. It is more friendly and trusting than a horse or pony foal, loving its owners only second to its mother. It looks enchanting, feels soft, warm and cuddly and smells of new — mown hay. It trots round the paddock on tiny high - heeled hooves and has its nose into everything from the day it is born.

But there are three disadvantages which must be considered carefu

Foals need a lot of time devoted to them when they are young. Jolly is being given a cuddle by his owner.

The first is that you will have to spend time looking after the mare for the twelve-month gestation period, foaling her down, and bringing up the baby for the first nine months. It is essential that she is supervised during foaling, and although the actual birth will only take about half an hour, unless you are expert you may be visiting her during the night for a week before she foals and you will probably be up most of the night when the baby is born.

You will have to see that the foal gets enough outdoor exercise without getting wet — some showery spring days we seem to be popping our mares and foals in and out all day. It is no good leaving the mare to take her foal in and out of an open shelter as she will go in herself but leave the foal playing outside in the rain. It must be realized therefore that someone will need to devote time to the mare and foal just before and for some time after the day of its birth.

The second point is that it will cost money. I am not going to try to give you an idea of the actual expenditure because prices will have altered before this is in print, but the costs involved include the stallion fee, keeping the mare at stud while she is being covered (mated), extra food for her for a year and for the mare and foal after foaling. You will possibly need to do some extra fencing to make a paddock foal-proof and you may have to make some alterations to their living quarters.

Finally, and most important of all, the foal is going to grow up! What are you going to do with it? Are you prepared to keep another donkey yourself? Even if it is a colt foal? It is lovely to own a donkey you have bred yourself and have known from birth, and it will have absolute trust in you; but there are times when space or economics prevent us keeping another grass-consuming mouth.

If you cannot keep the foal and do not know anyone who wants one *do not* put your mare in foal. There is no market for donkey foals unless they are prizewinning stock and have been prizewinners themselves. After all the care and love you have given to a little donkey it would break your heart to see it neglected in a bad home or passed from market to market, getting thin and wormy, with long feet and a defeated look in its eyes.

When a foal is born to your mare it becomes your responsibility for the rest of its life, which will be, we hope, thirty years or more.

Simon was a much loved foal. He has belonged to Maureen Gilmour since he was old enough to leave his mother twenty years ago and has had a wonderful life, looking after horses, driving, taking part in church festivities and going to shows.

Do not let this necessarily put you off having a donkey foal. What is needed is a long hard look into the future of your baby donkey before you take your mare to a stallion.

21 The Brood Mare

The first thing you must do when you decide to have a donkey foal is to join the Donkey Breed Society (where have we heard that before?) if you are not already a member. Then you will have the expert knowledge of the society to help you, you will be kept in touch with the donkey world through their magazines and newsletters and you will be able to buy their Stud Books and find out the details of the registered donkeys.

You will also be able to identify donkeys by their prefix. A prefix is an extra name which is given to all donkeys bred by one person or stud. Our prefix is Grove Hill. We bought our original donkey stock from Ruffs Orchard Donkey Stud who had imported them from Ireland and did not know any details of their parents. When they were sold to us we gave them Irish names and added the suffix 'of Grove Hill' - Barnabas of Grove Hill, Bridget of Grove Hill, etc. The foals of these donkeys were bred by us so we were entitled to put the prefix in front of the donkey's name - Grove Hill Menier, Grove Hill Trajan, Grove Hill Claudia, etc. We have registered our prefix with the Donkey Breed Society and nobody else is allowed to use it.

One does not need to be a stud or a big breeder to register a prefix; anyone who is a member of the D.B.S. may do so. Once you have registered your prefix your new foal will be known to have been bred by you. To register a prefix you choose a name, usually the name of your house or district, and send it to the Secretary of the D.B.S. with the small fee which is charged, and when it is approved no other person will be able to use that prefix but you. It is important to remember that the fact that a donkey has a prefix does not mean that it is necessarily in the D.B.S. Stud Book, but it is a good way of discovering the breeder or former owner.

If you do not have a donkey already make sure you buy one who is registered in the Stud Book. If you buy a young filly you have the advantage of knowing her sire and dam and if she comes from a reputable stud or a good home she will have had an excellent start in life in every way, but remember she must not be put in foal until she is at least three years old.

A young donkey is sometimes not as clever about looking after

A mare and her grown-up daughter taking turns to roll in the dust patch.

her first foal as an experienced mare. Should you decide to buy a mature mare, find out if she has foaled recently, and if she has not had a foal for three or four years try to find out why. Donkey mares can go on having foals without trouble until they are over twenty years old provided they have been having a foal regularly. By 'regularly' I mean every three or four years. I would not recommend putting a mare in foal for the first time if she were more than twelve to fourteen years old, but it does depend on her condition. If you are keen to have a foal from an older animal I suggest you have her examined by a veterinary surgeon to see if she is suitable for breeding.

An alternative is to get a mare already in foal. When she comes from a stud or a good private home this can be an excellent arrangement; but do make sure the vendor knows which stallion covered your mare, and the approximate foaling date, and get it in writing. Should a mare's owner have no idea who sired the foal be suspicious — it was probably a close relation; if she has foaled before it is possibly her son; if she is a young filly it is most likely a brother, half-brother or her father. In these cases any faults the mare has may be exaggerated in the foal.

A mare who is obviously in foal would cost half as much again for the foal; i.e. if the mare is worth £x empty, now she is in foal she is worth $£x + \frac{x}{2}$. If, however, she has only been covered recently the vendor should only charge the extra cost of the stud fee. This would depend on the stallion concerned — for that unknown relative I think the seller should knock something off the price.

If there is any possibility of having two mares to foal together it makes everything easier: they can go to stud together, giving each other confidence, they will be heavy in foal together and during the last few weeks when they are separated from other animals they can stay together and discuss their symptoms. Best of all the foals will play together, exercising each other and making much less work for you and their long-suffering dams.

Sometimes a foal will grow up very like her mother.

22 The Stallion

Any or all of the characteristics of the stallion you choose might be passed on to your foal, therefore he must have a perfect disposition, good conformation, and above all be free from any hereditary defect or disease; we can ensure the latter by choosing a stallion who is registered in the Stud Book.

Donkeys were so cross-bred in the past that it is impossible to be sure of the colour of a foal as it may take after a distant ancestor, and the height is determined by the mare (which is why a donkey stallion and a horse mare are used to breed large mules.) Even champion donkeys vary in conformation and you want one who will correct any weakness in your mare. For instance if you have a

D.B.S. Champion Barnabas at Ashford Hunt Show. Like all stallions he passes a number of his characteristics down to his progeny.

rather light-boned narrow mare with a pretty head, you would want a stallion with strong bone and a wide chest, but if your mare is one of those lovely big heavy-boned animals but with a slightly coarse head, you would need to look for quality rather than bone in your stallion.

Look up any stallion who interests you in the Stud Book and remember to take *all* his ancestors into consideration, not only the desirable ones; the foal is just as likely to take after his very plain grandmother as his champion grandfather.

You can assess him better by his progeny, so look them up too and see how many have been successful in the show ring.

You can judge a stallion's temperament by watching him at a

Barnabas in his winter coat at an early show. The fact that he is only tied by a halter and two young visitors are helping to groom him indicates his temperament.

show, and not only in the ring when his behaviour depends on his training and handling. If he is left tied up beside his box to be stroked and cuddled by the general public without supervision you can be sure he has a kind and placid disposition.

23 The Stud

If the stallion belongs to a stud which is registered with the D.B.S. you can be sure that your mare will be well cared for. If it is not registered ask whether she will be covered in hand or if the stallion runs with the mares. If she is served in hand it means that the mare will only be taken to the stallion when she is in season (oestrus) which is the only time she can conceive, and therefore the only time she will accept the stallion, and they will both be held while he serves her.

If the stallion runs with the mares — that is, the mares and the stallion are put together in a field and nature is allowed to take its course — you must ask more questions, and make absolutely certain she is only put in with him when she is in season. If she is put into a field with a stallion when she is not in season he will keep chasing her and as she cannot accept him she will run away and try to kick and fight him; if there are other mares with him they will become excited and join in the general affray. As you can imagine your mare is likely to get hurt, either by being kicked or by being so frightened she tries to burst through or jump over the surrounding fences.

Ask if your mare will be stabled separately at night and look at the field where she will graze to make sure it is clean, free from poisonous plants and safely fenced. Make sure there is a shelter in the field and not too many other donkeys to share it.

Ask, too, if any precaution is taken to prevent the stallion passing on infection from one mare to another.

Once you know she will be safe and have a happy time at the stud arrange with the owner when you would like her to be stocked (mated). You can have a donkey foal at any time of year and as the mare carries her foal for approximately twelve months calculation is simple.

A foal who is bred for showing will be at a disadvantage in the youngstock classes unless he is born early in the year: remember a donkey becomes a yearling on the next January 1st after his birth whatever his true birthday. However if you foal in February or March you will need a warm, draughtproof stable with some form of heating and you must be prepared to keep mare and foal under cover most of the first weeks, so they will need somewhere to exercise such as a covered yard or barn.

For this reason many people prefer April or May foalings when the grass is growing and the weather more reliable. Unfortunately this has a drawback too as it means that you will be weaning during the winter months when there is no good grass and the foal needs the warmth of his mother. If you are not particularly interested in showing him while he is young, consider having him in July or August: the mare has had the advantage of spring grazing and should be in top condition; by the time you are weaning, which will be in the spring if you keep him with his mother for nine months, he will be able to take advantage of the growing grass.

Make sure you and the stud owner are both clear about the business side of the proceedings and if possible have it in writing. He will quote a fee for stocking your mare and probably a small groom fee as well, plus a weekly charge for her keep.

Most studs offer a 'free return service'; this usually means that if the stallion has not put the mare in foal the stud will stock your mare again with the same stallion without charging a further fee. You will have to pay for her keep again while she is at stud, and you will be responsible for her travelling expenses. The stud will probably want to keep your mare for a further three weeks after she has been covered to make sure she is in foal. If, however, you live near, you might prefer to take her home and bring her back should she come into season again after three weeks. This is only practical if you can tell when she is in season.

It will help if you can tell the stud when your mare is due to come into season, then they can arrange for her to arrive a few days before to settle in. A donkey mare comes into season roughly every three weeks and when she is 'showing' she will lay back her ears and clamp her jaws as if she is chewing - she looks most unattractive - she might dribble a little and will often walk a few paces forward and then urinate. However not many donkeys are as demonstrative as this unless there is a stallion near.

The stud owner becomes fond of his visiting mares; he will try to make her as happy as possible, and not only because a contented mare is more likely to conceive.

A donkey mare in season making the usual mouths.

24 Preparing for a Foal

If the weather is sunny and warm and the mare foals during the day there is nowhere better for her to have her foal than in a smallish clean paddock, free from ditches and other hazards, where she can easily be supervised. Unfortunately donkeys usually have their foals at night so we must prepare a suitable stable or loosebox; there is no time of year when it is safe for a mare to foal out of doors at night in this country.

The foaling box should not be smaller than ten feet by eight feet. It must be clean and have no outstanding projections or crevices where the mare might get hurt or the foal catch his foot. These can be dealt with by stuffing and padding with straw. Bales of straw can guard a dangerous corner and another bale in front of the door will stop draughts and prevent the foal from getting caught under the door; but make sure the straw is still in place by the time the donkey foals and that she has not eaten it. If you are putting more than two bales on top of each other, tie them so that they cannot fall onto the mare or foal. The bucket of water will need to be placed where it cannot harm either mare or foal; we usually stand it on the ground in the corner with two bales of straw secured in front so that the mare can lean over to drink. The floor must be deeply strawed. The stable should have good ventilation yet be draught-free up to the height of the donkey.

You will need a clean paddock where the mare and foal can exercise, either near enough to her stable for them to use that as a shelter, or with a daytime shelter of its own, which needs a half-door so that they can be shut in when it rains. Pick up all the dung to prepare the field for the mare and foal and continue to pick it up every day while they are using it.

Should the mare be due to foal at any time other than midsummer put an infra-red heating lamp in the stable and turn on the light at night for about a week before you think she will foal; it will dry the air and the straw and if she catches you out and gives birth when you are not there she will be able to see the foal and avoid stepping on it. Should it be impossible to take electricity to the stable make sure you have at least one efficient torch with a new battery.

You will need an antibiotic to spray on the foal's navel as soon as the cord breaks, and, in the unlikely event of having to cut the cord, you will need a strong pair of blunt-ended scissors, some thin strong cord and a disinfectant to sterilize them and your hands. You are unlikely to need anything else other than warm towels to dry the baby if the mother fails to make a good job of it.

It is possible to be certain a mare is in foal by having her tested by a veterinary surgeon. Tests, however, can be expensive, and if she stops coming into season you can be reasonably sure she is in foal.

25 *The In-Foal Mare*

You will have between eleven and thirteen months to wait until your mare foals, and the way you look after her and feed her during this time will make a difference to the health and conformation of the foal.

A mare is pregnant from the time her egg (ovum) is fertilized by the sperm of the stallion; the mare and stallion contribute the same number of genes, and from this time the inherited characteristics of the foal are determined: sex, colour, type, temperament, etc. It is a fifty-fifty chance whether the foal will be a colt or a filly. When the embryo assumes a recognizable form, about forty days after fertilization, it is called a foetus and is about the size of a goose egg. The foetus is held inside two membranes which contain fluid, thus insulating it from shock or undue pressure. In this fluid lies the hippomane (which is soft and brownish and looks like a bit of liver) found only in equines and the object of much superstition and strange lore. Once thought to be carried in the foal's mouth, it is now known that it cannot be in contact with the foal, but its function is still not clearly understood.

The foetus depends entirely on its mother for protection and nourishment and the old saying, 'What is bad for the dam is bad for the foal,' is indeed true. Correct feeding is important throughout the pregnancy and essential during the last stage when the foal is growing rapidly. Remember that the mare, in the last weeks, as well as providing food for the unborn foal, will be developing the tissue of her udder. If the foetus should lack sufficient nourishment at any stage of pregnancy it may suffer a check in its growth. This might not be apparent in the size of the foal when it is born, especially if it occurs during the last few weeks of pregnancy, but it may have prevented its organs, such as heart, liver or kidneys from reaching a proper state of maturity. If the starvation occurs earlier in the pregnancy a foal will be small as well as immature when it is born.

This does not mean that you should overfeed your mare; the last thing you want is for her to get fat. If she puts on visible weight she also puts on fat inside, where it is not seen, but where it will compete with the foal for space and make a greater weight for her to carry. Give her two small feeds a day with a rather higher protein content than her usual feed, such as stud nuts, which are specially prepared for in-foal mares: 1½lb. at each feed would be

Moira shortly before she foaled. Her teats are visible as she grazes.

sufficient and, if you like, add a handful of dry bran. There are various vitamin and mineral additives you can put in her food; it is almost impossible to overdose her with the 'B' vitamins, but do not give her more cod liver oil than is prescribed. Make sure she has a salt lick.

During pregnancy she should have as much hay or straw as she likes to eat to deter her from eating too much grass, which is fattening and not nourishing except during its first growth. A dry diet will stop her from getting 'grass tummy', blown out by eating too much wet grass, which leaves less space for the foal.

She will need exercise. If she is usually driven or ridden let her continue to be so but do not overtire her. Remember that the weight of the unborn foal will be in addition to the weight of the rider and will be a strain on her backbone, so only let her carry a small child after the first six months. She can be quietly driven until about nine months. She will appreciate being taken for walks or shopping and if she enjoys showing and is not upset by travelling, continue to show her until her figure becomes unsuitable.

She will be putting extra weight on her feet so the farrier should see her regularly, and you should ask your vet to look at her teeth if they have not been checked recently.

Treat her for intestinal worms as soon as she returns from stud, making sure you use one of the anthelmintics that are safe to administer during the first months of pregnancy. Dose her again every three months but not after the tenth month. Treat her, too, against lungworm and keep a sharp look out for lice, which not only cause irritation but by sucking blood could make her anaemic.

If you have her injected against tetanus about a month before she foals she will pass on the immunity to her foal in the colostrum (the first milk) and the foal will not need to be injected against tetanus so early in his life.

You may find the mare's character changes. Her carefree youth is over and she will tend to become a little staid; not all the time — a good canter round the field will do her good. She is likely to be more affectionate, look after herself more carefully and, as the time for foaling approaches, she will want to be by herself or with you and away from the other animals. She will appreciate a little extra attention, longer grooming and deeper straw in her stable where she will lie down more than usual. She will expect you to understand that she is an important person.

26 *The Mare is About to Foal*

There is one question we are always being asked, 'How do you know when your donkey is about to foal?' Although it is not easy to tell, we have seldom missed the moment when the mare starts to give birth. And do not let anyone tell you that donkeys prefer to be left alone at this time; they do not — a loved and well cared-for mare has become your friend during the last year and she relies on you to look after her, to get help if necessary and to share her happiness when the foal is born.

A number of foals are lost every year because nobody was there to perform a small act such as removing the amnion (the bag) when it was entangled round the foal's nose. And if the foal is wrongly positioned the mare might be in labour, and in agony, all night and even die before help is available. It is your responsibility.

However, although we have seldom been late for the birth of a foal, I cannot count the number of times one of us has stayed up all night, visiting the mare every hour, to realize at dawn that she has no intention of foaling.

The first sympton you will see, telling you that her time is drawing near, is that the udder starts to swell. You will see her udder a little swollen one morning and by the evening it will be quite flat again. It gives little indication of her foaling date as some donkeys start to spring an udder two or three months before foaling and others leave it until the last two or three weeks of pregnancy, but it is time to shut her into the foaling box at night to give her time to get immune to any germs which are in the stable so that she will pass this immunity, with the colostrum, to her foal after it is born. She should be separated from any lively or troublesome animals but can still have a quiet friend with her.

Her udder will gradually increase in size and you will feel glands coming back from it towards her stomach. At first the teats will be small and close together, then as her udder swells they will appear to point inwards towards each other. As foaling draws nearer her udder will change noticeably, getting much larger, and the teats, now pointing straight downwards, will become swollen. Horses and ponies often get a wax-like substance at the end of their teats warning that birth is imminent; donkeys get this too, but I have known a donkey mare 'wax up' two weeks before she foaled.

Teena foaled the following day. He udder is already well up and the teats are beginning to swell.

When she is actually dripping milk you can be sure she will foal soon, and she should be checked every two hours, day and night. However some mares, especially maidens, do not develop much udder or swollen teats until after the foal is born. If you put your fingers round the base of her tail and squeeze gently and you find it soft she will soon give birth.

There is one certain indication she is about to foal: before she does she will expel all the dung out of her intestines. She will start dunging in the normal way, then you will find the faeces getting soft and she will dung more frequently. Soon she will be messy, not going to her usual place but standing or walking about anywhere in her stable or paddock expelling small pats of watery excretia. Now you can be almost sure she will foal during the next few hours (almost, because an upset digestion can show the same results). All this mess, together with a large udder and swollen teats, especially if she is standing with her tail held out and her vulva swollen, means the great moment is not far off. Visit her every half hour. Try not to disturb her, but if you are unable to reconnoitre without her knowing you are there it is better to talk to her gently as you approach.

27   *The Birth of a Foal*

The birth of a donkey foal can be divided into three stages: first the start of contractions of the uterus up to the time when the 'water' breaks, secondly the expulsion of the foal from its mother and thirdly the dropping of the afterbirth.

FIRST STAGE

The mare will become restless. She is suffering intermittent pain from contractions and she will appear uneasy, walking about rapidly, then relaxing and perhaps nibbling some hay or grass, then walking about again. She will probably want to keep away from other animals but may become affectionate towards you. The duration of this stage varies from about thirty minutes to a few hours. At the end of the first stage the placenta (the outer membrane) ruptures and the allantonic fluid escapes, but the amnion (the inner membrane) still remains unbroken.

We see this breaking of the water as a stream of brownish-coloured fluid coming from the vulva. We are told ways of distinguishing this from a donkey urinating, but I do not think the two could possibly be confused as so much allantonic fluid comes out with such a rush.

SECOND STAGE

Now the expulsion of the foal has started, so check the time by your watch. She will start to strain and will lie down and stand up again several times. Within half an hour the amnion will start to protrude from the mare's vulva (she may be lying down or standing up, it does not matter), often looking like a small white balloon. She will continue to strain at intervals and soon one front foot of the foal, with a covering of white gristle, will be seen inside the bag. Next you will see the second foot, slightly behind the first, and then after a few minutes the foal's nose — his tongue will probably be hanging out of his mouth. During this time the mare may have stood up and flopped down several times — do not worry; she will not actually sit on the protruding foal. Now she will probably lie on her side and strain, possibly stretching her head back and even baring her teeth. She is making a tremendous effort to get the shoulders of the foal through the opening in her pelvis. Usually it emerges gradually, inch by inch, as she strains. Unless you are an expert and know about delivering foals or calves do nothing to help her, except to talk to her soothingly, until the foal's shoulders are out of her vulva.

By the time the foal's head and shoulders are showing he will probably have broken the amnion by struggling with his front feet, but if it is still covering his head tear the membrane apart at his nose so that his head is free, and make sure his nose cannot fall into dirt or water. Throughout pregnancy the foal's oxygen supply has come from the mare through the umbilical cord but now he is beginning to breathe through his own lungs and there must be no obstruction; if he breathes fluid into his lungs he will drown.

At this stage the mare often rests before expelling the hindquarters of the foal. She usually lies on her side, with the head and shoulders of the foal protruding from her vulva, and you can see she is resting and not straining. Soon she will start to strain again, slowly expelling the back half of the foal. Sometimes she will stand up, even walk about, with the foal projecting from her vulva, but she will probably lie down again before the last of the foal slithers out, often followed by a gush of discoloured water.

The foal's feet and lower part of his legs will usually remain in the mare's vagina. Leave the foal where he is while he is quiet, but if he starts to kick about we like to free his back legs and feet, pulling carefully *downwards* (this is important) towards her hocks. Being very, very careful not to break the umbilical cord, we move him gently round towards the mare's head so that she can see him, and even lick him, without having to stand up.

This umbilical cord has supplied blood to the foal during pregnancy and continues to do so for five or ten minutes after he starts to breathe with his lungs; then the circulation through the cord stops naturally, leaving all the blood in the foal. If the cord is broken or cut prematurely the blood which is in the placenta is wasted as the foal loses it. So you can see that care should be taken to keep the umbilical cord intact. If the mare foals standing up, unless the afterbirth comes away with the foal, the cord usually breaks and some of the blood is lost. Should this happen watch the foal carefully for the first few days and if he seems listless ask your vet to come and see him.

Usually after the mother and foal have rested for about ten

A mare and newly born foal still joined by the umbilical cord.

minutes either the mare stands up or the foal starts to struggle and the cord breaks near the foal's navel, where there is a natural place for it to rupture, causing no bleeding.

I have known the umbilical cord refuse to break. Should this happen, you will have to cut the cord: do not worry, it is simple. The procedure is to soak a pair of sturdy, blunt-ended scissors and some thin but strong cord in water to which you have added disinfectant and to wash your hands in disinfectant too. Wind the string tightly round the umbilical cord about one inch from the foal and tie tightly; then cut the umbilical cord about half an inch further from the foal, between the tie and the mare, so that the ligature round the cord remains on the foal. There should be very little blood, if any. Do not leave more of the cord hanging down than is necessary as this dead tissue can cause infection, or, if it is very long, it may get caught on the straw and pull on the foal's navel.

Whether the umbilical cord has broken naturally, as it is almost sure to do, or you have cut it, you *must* spray the stump of the cord left at the foal's navel with an antibiotic powder or spray *immediately*. This is the most vulnerable entry for germs to attack the foal, and this is one more reason why you must be present at the birth.

THIRD STAGE

Now you have to wait for the mare to stand up and 'cleanse' (the afterbirth comes away) and the foal to get to his feet and have a drink. Usually the mare is first to get up and she will have the umbilical cord and the empty amnion hanging from her vulva. Do not on any account pull out the afterbirth; if she has not dropped it after three or four hours, or by morning if she has foaled during the night, call your veterinary surgeon.

To expel the afterbirth she will stretch her legs as if she is going to urinate, strain, and it will slither out. Clear it away as soon as you can, as sometimes it distracts her, and put down fresh straw trying to make as little dust as possible. While you are tidying up the stable do search for that mysterious hippomane. Hang it up to dry (no fly will go near it) and it will bring you and your donkeys good fortune.

The expulsion of the afterbirth marks the end of the third stage

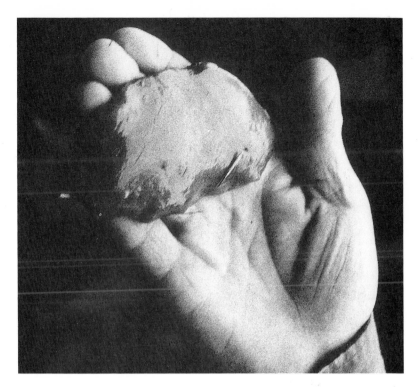

The mysterious hippomane. It is considered lucky to find it at the birth of a foal and it used to be dried and kept as it was believed to have magical properties.

of the birth but the mare has waste matter and liquid in her uterus which needs to be excreted. Exercise during the first days after foaling including rolling will help discharge this waste matter, and so will having a good loud bray, which uses the appropriate muscles.

It is essential that the mare should have somebody with her while she is foaling to check all is well and summon help if necessary, but she will strongly object to an audience. Do not let the family, neighbours, or doubtful 'experts' disturb her. Her owners, and, if necessary, a vet, are the only people who should be present.

WHEN TO CALL THE VETERINARY SURGEON

When we first had donkeys we were so nervous when a mare foaled we summoned our veterinary surgeon as soon as she started in labour. As the practice was a little way from us the vet usually arrived about the same time as the foal. In spite of being called out unnecessarily in the middle of the night he was always charming and would check the afterbirth and admire the foal.

Veterinary books give diagrams of all the wrong positions in which a foal can be presented (upside down, back to front, etc.) so that you would wonder if your foal had any chance of being born naturally, but I do assure you it is almost certain that he will be.

Once the water has broken and the mare is in labour she will probably produce her foal within thirty minutes. If there appears to be undue delay at any stage of foaling, and by undue delay I mean about half an hour, call your vet. Thirty minutes can seem to last for ever if you are worrying about your donkey, and this is why I say check the time she starts.

One of the most common causes of death in a foal is that there is nobody present to make sure he can get his first breath without obstruction. Another cause of death is infection entering the foal through an unsprayed navel.

28 *The Newborn Foal*

It must be a tremendous shock to be born. In a matter of minutes the foal is surrounded by air instead of being suspended in fluid and is in an environment that is probably at least 40 F. lower than he has been used to. He has to breathe with his lungs for the first time, suck, swallow and digest his food, and support himself on his legs. We must do all we can to help him. In nature the tribulations of birth sort out the weak from the strong, but we want to make sure our foal will survive.

Within minutes of his birth the foal will start to try to get to his feet. These movements will encourage deeper breathing, and falling back onto the straw during his efforts will slap more air into his lungs. His legs will appear to bend in all directions but eventually he will balance and start looking for his mother's milk in the wrong places, especially between her front legs. He can be exasperating, but if she has had foals before the mare will soon push him into the correct position. If this is her first foal it might take some time, but

Tarquinia when she was first born before she had her ears up. Now she is the mother of champions and she and her owner, Austen Knibb, who is Area Representative for Sussex, take part in most varied activities including giving rides to disabled children.

provided he gets up when he falls down and has the energy to keep searching do not worry.

If the foal is shivering this is nature's way of trying to keep warm, but it does indicate that he is cold, so rub him well with warm towels, not forgetting his chest and legs — we have found donkeys useless about licking their foals dry. When his ears stand up he is well and comfortable. Check that everything in the stable is safe and leave them for at least half an hour. By this time you will need refreshment too.

Moira is an exception in that she is a great licker. She not only licks her own foals but any others and even her owners.

The first milk a foal gets from his mother is called colostrum and it is vital for his health, possibly for his survival. Many animals, including humans, give birth to their young with immunity already acquired from their mothers, but with equines antibodies are produced in the colostrum and until these are absorbed by the foal's stomach with his first feed he is unprotected from infection. When you return to the stable you should be able to tell if he has had his first drink. If he is still sniffing round his mother, and mouthing, go away again for a while — it will not hurt him if he does not drink immediately. Once he has had a feed he will

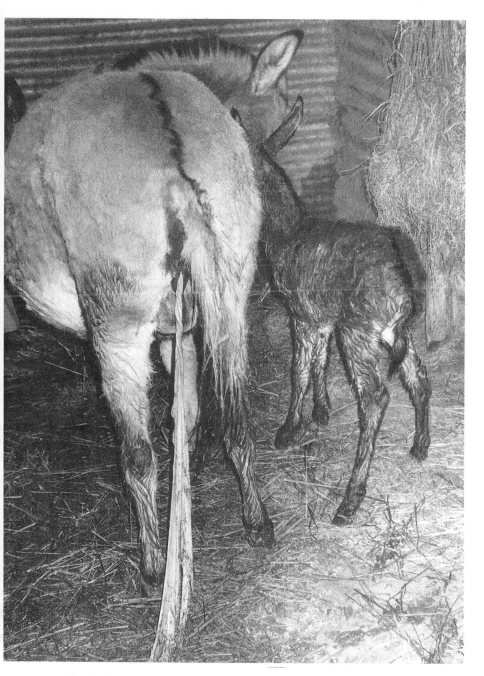

The foal is just born and Justinia has the empty amnion hanging from her vulva. Her udder is large and swollen.

probably lie down,but he will soon get up again and have another drink and this time be more expert at finding his mother's udder.

It is only if he falls down and does not bother to get up, or stops mouthing and searching, that you need to help. First get him on his feet again and try to move him gently into position. Should he still refuse to drink, or if the mare will not let him suckle, you will have to get some milk from the mare and feed him with it; fortunately this is seldom necessary. If you do have to feed him remember that a donkey's temperature is approximately 101°F. and the milk must be this temperature when the foal drinks it.

Heat a baby's bottle, or any other bottle that will take a teat, and a funnel, both should have been disinfected either by boiling or by using one of the preparations sold for sterilizing babies' bottles;

Kathleen, an experienced mare, is nudging the newly born Caligular into position to drink.

warm by rinsing them in hot boiled water and wrap the bottle in a warm towel to maintain the temperature. Then milk the mare directly into the bottle using the funnel. If she is restless and objects to being milked, get someone to lift one of her front legs; she cannot kick or walk about on three legs. You will probably need to enlarge the hole in the artificial teat for the foal to drink; he will only need a couple of tablespoonfuls to start with. Only let him suck a little at a time and give him plenty of opportunity to swallow. If he is still uninterested and seems languid you must send for your vet. *Never* give a newly born foal anything to drink other than his mother's milk at the correct temperature until he has been examined by your veterinary surgeon.

Once the foal has had his first drink the mare would probably like a small feed of her usual dry food and a fresh haynet. It is often suggested that you should give the mare a warm bran mash after she has foaled; we find that, apart from Moira, ours do not like bran mashes — perhaps I am particularly inept at producing tasty ones. When our first foals started to arrive I hopefully made one for each mare, which was always refused, and Moira had lovely extra night-time feeds of cool bran mashes. We do find, however, that the mare appreciates a bucket of lukewarm water to drink.

When you are sure the foal is feeding regularly — he will probably drink every half an hour at first — leave them alone together for two or three hours. If he is born during the night leave them until the morning, but if he is born in the evening I would suggest a visit during the night to make sure all is well. Leave the light on even if they do not need the warmth so that the mare can see the foal.

29 *The Growing Foal*

Foals are splendid time-consumers and you can quiet your conscience when you are neglecting other duties by remembering that both mother and baby will benefit from attention in the first few days. When you go into the stable speak to the mare and make a fuss of her. Then sit down on a bale of straw and call the foal by name. He will be so full of curiosity he will be unable to resist coming to you. Do not stretch out your hand above his eyes, but tickle him under his chin, scratch his chest and the top of his rump. Talk to him all the time and keep saying his name. This is the start of training.

Keep the stable immaculate, removing the mare's dung as often as necessary, and make sure she has as much good hay as she wants and that she always has clean drinking water. She needs extra fluid when she is making milk and can be encouraged to drink by being given tepid water if she prefers it. She will need the same food as she had when she was carrying the foal.

It is reassuring to know the foal is dunging properly. During pregnancy the waste products of the baby which cannot be eliminated through the mare's placenta are stored in the foal's bowels until after he is born. These foetal faeces are called meconium and are dark greeny-brown, usually in the form of pellets coated with a sticky paste. This has to be evacuated before the first of the mare's milk can pass through. The dung from the mare's colostrum, called milk dung, is quite different in appearance, usually like a sort of yellow or orange paste. Although it is always satisfactory to find the meconium, do not worry; if he is not getting rid of his waste matter satisfactorily he will soon let you know that he is in discomfort and you must call your vet. The same applies to seeing him urinate: it is nice to know all is well, but he will let you know quickly if he is in pain.

Unless it is raining or there is a bitterly cold wind, take the mare and the foal out into the paddock to exercise as soon as the dew is off the grass. The mare needs to roll and the foal must learn to use his lungs and stretch his legs. If it is cold or the grass is wet bring them back to their stable as soon as the foal tires and wants to lie down. In unpleasant weather several short outings are better than one long one. On warm sunny days they can stay out until late afternoon.

To lead the foal from place to place hold him under the chin with your left hand, to guide him, and push his rump gently with your right hand. If you get somebody to lead the mare he will soon get the idea. Should you need to carry the foal you must pick him up with one arm under his rump, pushing his back legs forward, and with the other arm under his chest, pushing his front legs backwards. Never lift him with your hand or arm between his legs so that his weight is on his rib-cage or abdomen.

The foal's hair soaks up water and he will get chilled if you allow him out in the rain or to lie down on wet grass. Every time there is a shower he must be shut with his mother in a shelter. Foals are prone to both enteritis and pneumonia.

The mare will need grooming, but wait until she is outside to avoid making dust in the stable. Look at her vulva to see if it is split or dirty and if necessary wash it with warm salt water — you

The correct way to pick up a foal. Although he is only two days old Justavius is quite an armful.

will find it heals quickly. Look at the mare's udder each morning
and evening and watch the foal when he is drinking. His mother
should stand for him to suckle and when he leaves her he should
appear contented and probably lie down to sleep. If he keeps going
back to her every few minutes, butting her with his head, it means
he is not getting enough milk. Never give him artificially made-up
milk as an addition to his mother's milk or you will certainly upset
his stomach; instead encourage the mare to produce more milk by
giving her extra food and water. Of course if he is really underfed,
and is getting listless, you must call your vet and follow his
instructions.

Her udder should be an even shape and be soft, warm and
flexible to touch, and she should not object to the foal suckling or
to you touching her udder. If it appears lopsided, feels hot and
hard, or seems tender, or if she persistently pushes her foal away,
you will have to contact your vet immediately as she might have
mastitis. Ask him to come as soon as possible as the earlier mastitis
is treated the easier it is to cure. In general do not worry if you see
her push the foal away now and again; she is only teaching him
regular habits.

The foal will not need any food other than the mare's milk for a
few weeks although you may see him pretending to nibble the grass
or even pulling a wisp of hay from the net. Foals are born without
teeth but within the first three or four days his front teeth will start
to come through and he will celebrate by biting everything he can.
Discourage him from biting you. Some foals acquire the unpleasant
habit of eating their mother's dung. We are assured it does no
harm, but I hate to see it. Reprimanding the foal will frighten him
and the only cure is to pick up the dung before he finds it.

The most prevalent illness to which foals are subject is
scouring,or diarrhoea. Diarrhoea occurs when the foal is unable to
digest his food satisfactorily and the bacteria, which is always
present in all healthy intestines, multiply and infect the walls of his
bowels which become inflamed. This can be caused by unsuitable
food, such as substituted milk, by severe chilling or by infection.
The foal's dung acquires a distinctive odour and he soon becomes
listless and either refuses to drink or drinks excessively. You must
call your veterinary surgeon urgently so that he can treat the foal
before he gets too weak. Donkey foals have little resistance to

If he has no companion of his own age a foal will play with his mother;
Antonius gave Teena a lively time.

illness and it could be difficult to save his life, so do not wait to see
if he is better in the morning.

When the mare comes into season for the first time after foaling
it will affect her milk and the foal will probably get slightly loose,
but this has no distinctive smell and seldom causes listlessness.

Any sign of a cold or heavy breathing is another signal that your
vet is needed and you must get him quickly. Watch the foal
carefully if you think he might have got chilled; pneumonia needs
to be treated early. I am happy to say you are unlikely to have
trouble with your foal's health if he is kept clean, dry, free from

draughts, and exercised as often as possible in the sunshine. Every day he will grow and put on weight and he will be a great joy.

Soon he will start to eat out of his mother's food bowl and you will have to separate them when they are feeding to make sure he gets his fair share. Let him have as much as he wants twice a day —he will not overeat. He will soon eat grass and hay too but his main nourishment is his dam's milk for at least nine months so do not wean him earlier. Make sure the bucket of drinking water in the stable is low enough for him to drink from — it will eventually make weaning easier. Check, too, that he can reach the salt lick. As he gets older you will need to double their hay ration.

When he is a few months old you will find he eats more than the

An overweight donkey can lose her figure when in foal and become dipped in the back

mare, which is not surprising when you think of teenagers, and he needs this good food to grow and make bone. He should be wormed for the first time at about four weeks old and then every six weeks for the first two years; intestinal worms are particularly damaging to young animals. Worm your mare too, a couple of weeks after the foal is born and at six-weekly intervals while they are together.

Start brushing him gently when he is a few days old and lift his feet every day so that he becomes used to having his hooves handled. When your farrier comes to attend to the mare's feet ask him to look at the foal's feet too. The farrier will know when they need attention and meantime the foal will make friends with him.

Be careful not to neglect the mare for the foal. Always speak to her first and let her know she is your favourite donkey.

30   Weaning

Weaning, everybody will tell you, is a nasty business; distressing because you are causing both the mare and the foal a certain amount of anguish, and on the mare's part physical pain. However it is possible to manage separation of mother and youngster in such a way that minimal suffering is inflicted on either. Most important is not to wean too soon; a young donkey should be weaned much later than a horse or pony foal. In the desert the wild donkey mares leave the herd to foal, and stay away for some months, consequently breeding only every second year, and they feed their foals for anything up to eighteen months!

We find that when a foal reaches about ten months or a year the mare will often wean him herself, thus relieving the owner, the mare and the young donkey of any anxiety, but if the mare is already in foal again, or if you must wean him earlier for some reason, never do so before six months. I have seen healthy foals who have been weaned at five months having to be hand-fed with milk and water because they had become dehydrated since they had been used to getting their liquid from the mare.

If you have more than one donkey you can start by separating mare and youngster either at night or during the day only, but you need another animal to keep the foal company when he is not with his mother. We always do this and find they quickly get used to waiting until they meet for the foal to have a drink. You will be surprised how small her udder is in a month's time.

When the mare and foal are finally parted they must not be able to see or hear each other for three weeks, and unless you have plenty of land the simplest way is to send one or other away. A friend might enjoy having the mare for the school holidays, or if you wish to have another foal she could be sent to stud — we find a mare 'takes' well on her weaning season.

If the foal is going to a new home this is the time for him to leave you.

Some responsible person will need to look at the mare's udder twice a day to make sure it goes down evenly and does not get hard or sore. It is sure to get a little swollen at first, but it is unlikely she will have trouble unless her foal is weaned too early. Should her udder get painful or lopsided the vet must be sent for immediately.

Do not shut up the poor mare with dry food and Epsom salts in her water as she would hate it, and have nothing to do all day except worry about her foal, and anxiety is bad for her at this time. On the other hand do not put her in a field of spring grass that would stimulate milk production. Keep her busy and as happy as possible.

After three weeks mare and young donkey can be reunited. The youngster will probably look for a drink out of habit, but there will be nothing there and his mother will reprimand him for being cheeky. Soon they will be good companions and when he has been gelded (if a male) she will have a delightful friend and a playmate for her next foal.

31 *Hand-Rearing a Foal*

If you are hand-rearing a foal and can milk the mother to feed him for at least the first day it will make all the difference to your chance of success as he will receive immunity from infections from her colostrum. Should the mare's colostrum be unobtainable the foal will require injections to help protect him.

Immediately after he is born the foal must be dried thoroughly with warm towels and kept warm by keeping his infra-red lamp on to dry the atmosphere and the straw. A really thick carpet of straw can generate heat and cut down draughts. If it is winter make him a jacket from a thick blanket or thick towel.

The easiest way to bring up a foal who is totally rejected by his mother, or perhaps orphaned, is to find another donkey mare who will feed him. Try telephoning your local donkey stud; but remember that even if he is adopted by another mare he will need, if it is in any way possible, his own mother's colostrum for, at least one day. If you are unsuccessful in finding a foster mother he will have to be fed by hand. When analysed donkey milk was found to be nearer to human milk than that of any other animal, even horses and ponies. Years ago delicate human babies were given donkey milk, and the late Reggie Summerhays, the first President of the D.B.S., could actually remember a London establishment housing fifty donkey mares, each yielding a quart of milk per day, for delicate babies. Customers either bought the milk or hired a donkey.

Donkey milk is low in butter fat and high in sugar so Ostermilk with added glucose is a good substitute. I would not recommend diluted cow's milk, or the often suggested goat's milk, as the butter fat content is too high. There is a powdered milk sold for feeding horse foals but it is not as suitable as simulated human milk.

A recipe using Ostermilk is:
10 fluid oz. boiled water
8 level measures Ostermilk (the measure is supplied)
2 tablespoons of glucose (make sure it is fresh)
   To be fed at a temperature of 101°F.

You will have to feed the foal day and night at two-hourly intervals for the first week and this is a time-consuming but rewarding undertaking. To start with he will probably only take 2 or 3 ounces at each feed, and ideally should be fed hourly for the first eight hours, gradually increasing the interval to two hours, by which time he should be taking from 4 to 6 ounces. Always let him have as much as he wants and do not hurry him.

An orphaned foal will be lonely unless he can be found a companion.

When he is drinking well you will be able to cut down the number of feeds during the night and at three weeks, if he is strong and healthy, he should be able to go onto three-hourly feeds during the day and four-hourly intervals at night; eventually you will be able to cut out the night feed altogether,when he is obviously healthy and eating well. Always keep to the same milk food and do not change recipes or you will upset his stomach, and always feed at the temperature of 101°F. Sterilize all the feeding equipment regularly. Make up his milk freshly for each feed and throw away any he leaves.

Fresh water should be kept in his stable.

As soon as possible — try first at three weeks — encourage him to eat a little hard food in addition to the liquid. A mixture of equal parts broad bran, crushed oats and flaked maize would be suitable. Start him on half a handful three times a day fed dry. A vitamin supplement could be useful but consult your vet about this as he may prefer to inject vitamins. Any supplement must be introduced gradually to his diet.

Put a little good hay into his stable from three or four weeks and let him nibble the grass in his paddock.

You must continue to keep him warm, especially at night, and if you have another donkey, a goat or other friendly animal let them stay together for company. You might be able to borrow a kindly donkey to be with him — not necessarily a mare; geldings make good nursemaids too.

When he is five months old you could start to wean him if he is well grown. Do it gradually, cutting out one milk meal per day each week and increasing his ration of hard food. Give him all the good hay he likes to eat and three feeds of cereal weighing about 1 lb. (three handfuls) at each meal every day. Diminish or increase the amount to suit his appetite — he will not overeat at his age. Remember he must have clean water both in his stable and paddock — you cannot stop giving him milk until he has learned to drink water.

You may find, as he gets older, that he will drink directly from a bowl, and you can dispense with the bottle.

Much work and patience is needed to hand-rear a foal but there is tremendous satisfaction to be found in achieving your goal and you will have a special rapport with him all his life.

A DEAD FOAL

There is also the sad possibility that the foal is born dead or dies. If this happens it is important to leave the foal with his mother for half an hour so that she can realize he is dead. She will then accept the situation and will not remain upset for long. If you take the foal away too quickly she will think he is still alive and has been stolen from her and will be frantic. Once she realizes her foal is dead her udder will dry quickly; your vet may suggest giving her an injection to reduce her milk supply if he thinks it necessary. Keep her feeding down to a minimum without making her fretful and don't allow her to eat any rich grass, but do let her drink as much water as she pleases. Check her udder regularly but don't on any account milk her or you will stimulate her into making more. Above all keep the mare as happy as possible; what she needs is kindness and company. If you have another donkey, put them together and spend as much time with her as you can yourself.

If this was your mare's first foal ask your vet for advice about putting her in foal again. He will know if the foal's death was due to any defect he might have inherited or if it was just bad luck, and he will tell you if she could be stocked during her first season, or, if she has had a bad time foaling, if it would be better to let her recover for a few months or even wait until the following year.

32 The Elderly Donkey

When an equine reaches the age of ten years it is termed 'aged' because it is less easy to tell its exact age by its teeth. At ten years old a donkey is in the prime of life, perfect for every type of activity. Donkeys start to creak a little and are past their best in the show ring when they are twenty, and are in need of a little cossetting by the time they are in their thirties.

The oldest donkey we have ever cared for was Sally, who belonged to a friend of ours but lived with us for years. She was not really old when she died, only in her early thirties, but some donkeys seem to age sooner than others. She completely gave up eating or drinking and died peacefully having decided the time had come. Our vet said it would be wrong to distress her by forcible feeding to keep her alive for our, not her, pleasure and assured us she was in no pain or discomfort. Fortunately we were having a rare spell of sunny weather and she would amble out of her stable when the grass was dry and lie down in the sunshine. She lasted longer than any of us expected, and one day when we had a foal who was having her first outing in the next paddock Sally walked over to the fence and kissed her. She seemed to watch her with interest all day, but in the evening my husband reported that she was reluctant to get up and he thought we might need some help to get her into her stable, and before help arrived, while he was sitting on the grass beside her, she stopped breathing.

No matter how prepared one is it is still sad to lose an old friend, and every time we passed her stable (she lived in a special loose box which was part of the feeding barn, known as the Snuggery) we missed her and never put another donkey in her stable.

She, like many elderly donkeys, suffered from arthritis. At one time it became painful and our vet treated her with such success that although she was always a little stiff in one leg she never seemed to be in pain again. She always walked with a slight limp, and objected to standing on three legs to have her feet trimmed, so she used to have the hoof on her arthritic leg trimmed while she stood and then lie down to have the others attended to. People have said to me that they think it is cruel to keep a donkey alive if she suffers from arthritis, but I suffer from it too, and I am not

Sally was quite old when she had Fleur, and needed veterinary help at the birth, but all was well and Fleur grew up to be a beautiful mare.

ready to be put down yet.

One thing we thought helped her was giving her a tablespoon of cider vinegar in her food every day, and she loved to have her bad leg massaged by my husband, but whether it was the rubbing or just the attention she enjoyed I am not sure.

Elderly donkeys, like elderly people, need to be kept active and interested in life. They still enjoy going for a walk, even if it needs to be a shorter and more level outing, and they are much less trouble to have in the kitchen when they are old, and tether better on the lawn. Even the oldest donkey can manage a tiny child on his back for a few minutes, and will love a visit from children who are kind and gentle. I think when donkeys are *really* old it is permissible to give tit-bits; they are not going to retain any bad habits for long, alas.

Older donkeys need more warmth — an infra-red lamp in their stable on cold nights is welcome — and so is really deep soft straw, both for warmth and to ease rheumatic bones, as they are not so agile and sink more heavily when they are getting down to rest. They do like the sun on their backs, but must have shelter from flies. Sally always wore a fly-veil in summer.

An older donkey eats rather less than a young one, but still needs nourishment in an easily digested form and certainly benefits from a vitamin and mineral supplement. Ponynuts may be rather hard for his teeth, so put him on a mixture of one part bran, one part rolled oats (you are not likely to make him too lively) and one part flaked maize. Keep the food dry as long as possible; if he is really aged he might need his food to be soaked. An old donkey is often rather thin, but this is better than being too fat with the subsequent strain on his legs and feet. If he is greatly overweight it is too late to slim him now so give him a normal amount of food. Elderly donkeys enjoy eating succulent grass and herbs but can overdo it, just like any donkey. A slow walk down a lane with interesting hedges will give him exercise and a delectable treat at the same time.

His teeth are of utmost importance to him and will be worn out of shape, so get your vet to examine them and file them if necessary twice a year. While he is attending him for his teeth suggest a multi-vitamin injection, which seems to have a rejuvenating effect. And do not forget he still needs his anti-tetanus and influenza injections and his regular worming.

Like all donkeys he needs a well ventilated stable but let him wear a warm coat at night during the winter months. He will still need a little outdoor exercise every day, even when it is cold, but he can keep his rug on. An old donkey should be brushed every day and if he is wearing a rug day and night it is particularly important, not only to make sure it fits him well and is comfortable, and that none of the straps or fastenings rub him, but to take it off twice a day while you groom him, and smooth his hair the right way when you put it on again. Old donkeys are even more prone to lice than younger ones and lice live happily under a warm rug, so treat him spring and autumn even if you can see no sign of infestation and keep an eagle eye for parasites all year round.

A donkey who has had pneumonia in his youth, or a bad infestation of lungworm at any time, is likely to show it more once he is old. If his breathing is bad you might need to keep his hay damped and use peat for bedding instead of straw. Quick breathing, or a rasping sound, is an indication that all is not well and you should get your vet to visit him and suggest a routine for his old age.

In some ways elderly donkeys are a little more work to look after than those in their prime of life but in other ways they are less trouble, as they behave in a placid and serene manner, are less likely to be boisterous or impetuous, and seem more affectionate and grateful for anything you do for them; I think perhaps they are the most lovable of all donkeys.

33 *Parting*

Our best laid plans can go astray, and it might be impossible for you to keep your donkey until the end of his life. Circumstances change and perhaps you cannot have a house with land, or due to your own ill health or old age you feel you cannot look after him satisfactorily any longer. It is sad to part with an old friend who has put his trust in you and you must plan well ahead and do nothing in a hurry.

You might get a good home for him through the Area Representative of the Donkey Breed Society, or your vet might know of somebody who is looking for a donkey and whom he knows would provide the kind of life your donkey is accustomed to. If you have a good donkey stud near you get in touch with them, as studs often have enquiries for pet donkeys which they are unable to supply.

Whatever home you consider sending him to you must go and visit it, and have a good talk with his prospective owners, as this is the only way you can have an easy mind about him and how he will be cared for.

If you are unable to find a home which you consider suitable, or if he is very old, or needs some kind of special attention, get in touch with the Donkey Sanctuary. Once they have taken responsibility for him you need have no worry about his future. If they think he is suitable they may let him live in a private home, but he will always belong to them, and they will send an inspector to see him at regular intervals to make sure he is being well looked after.

Do not sell him to a dealer or in a market or you will have no control over his future at all and he may end up unloved and neglected or possibly sold on for pet food.

Due to old age or ill health it may be necessary to have your donkey put to sleep. This can be done painlessly on your own premises, so that he is peaceful and cherished until the end. Do not let him be taken to a slaughterhouse, where, although they might treat him with every consideration, he could be kept waiting for some time before he is shot, and he might get very frightened and upset in a strange place without friends. If you have him put to sleep in his own stable or paddock he can be happy and confident until the end of his life.

Index

Figures in bold type indicate illustrations

Abscesses 100, 101
Aconitum 33
Acorns 33
Administering medicine 102
Afterbirth 131, 132, **137**
Age 10-11, 74, 81
Aged 81, 150
Allantonic fluid 129
Allergies 107
Amnion 129-32, **137**
Angelina **16**
Anthelminitics 25, 90-93 :
  administering 91
Anti-flu injections 26, 100 :
  elderly donkey 153
Anti-fly ear tags 97
Anti-histamine injection 107
Anti-tetanus injections 26,
  87, 100 : elderly donkey
  152
Antibiotics 87, 98, 100, 101,
  104, 132 : spray or
  powder 105, 110, 111,
  123, 132, 134
Antonius **143**
Anus 105, 106
Appetite (loss of) 104, 110
Appia Via **32**
Apples 33, 45
Approaching a donkey 29,
  140
Argentia **38**
Arrival at new home 27-30
Arthritis 152-2
Ashford Hunt Show **118**
Aureomycin 88

Back **19**, 109 : conform-
  ation **20**, 21
Back end 105
Backing (reversing) 63
Back legs **19** : conformation
  22
Barbed wire 35

Bare patches on skin 94, 108
  see also Hair falling out
Barley straw 39
Barnabas **16**, 18, **36**, 63,
  118, 119
Bedding 39
Beet *see* Sugar beet
Bendazole 93
Benzyl benzoate 108, 109,
  111
Best condition and turnout
  class 76
Birth of a foal 113, 129 :
  first stage 129; second
  stage 129; third stage 132;
  symptoms 133; undue
  delay 134 *see also* Foal
Bit 48, 49, 50, 74 : size 50
Biting 60, 64, 90
Black donkeys 15, **16**
Black-nosed donkeys 18
Blackthorn 35
Blanket *see* Donkey rug
Blinkers (driving) 73
Blocked tear duct **98**, 98-9
Bluebells 34
Body brush 51
Bog itch 95, 106
Borwick, The Hon. Robin
  23, 26
Bot fly 93, 105 : eggs 93
Bottle feeding 138, 147
Bramble 33
Bran 44` : bran mash 139
Breaking a donkey 66, 70
Breast harness 71
Breathing quickly 101, 110 :
  with difficulty 107, 110;
  foal 143; foal's first
  breath 130, 131; elderly
  donkeys 153 *see also*
  Pneumonia
Breeching (harness) 72
Breeding 12, 112-49

Bridget **16, 23-4, 26**
Bridle 48, 75, 78 : for
  driving 73 : putting on 49
Broken-coloured donkeys 15
Browband 48
Bruises 104
Brushing *see* Grooming
Bulgarian donkeys 18
Bumps and lumps 108, 111
Buttercups 33, 44
Buying hay and straw 42
Bryonies 33

Caligula **138**
Campbell, Dr Marcus 72
Canker 95
Cannon **19**, 22
Care, Bill **43**
Carrots 45
Cart *see* Vehicle
Castlecrete Donkey Stud **43**
Castration 12, 24
Cattle and sheep 90
Cereal 25, 29 : amount 44
Championship Show
  (D.B.S.) 74
Chapping 95, 106, 107
Chest **19**, 101 :
  conformation 21
Children's Riding Class **68**,
  74
Chill 101, 107 : foal 141,
  142, 143
Choosing a donkey 9-18
Cider vinegar 15
Cleansing (afterbirth) 132
Clipping a donkey 94
Clover 33, 89
Cold 99, 101 : foal 143
Colic 30, 45, 101-103
Collecting ring 78
Colostrum 126, 127, 136,
  146
Colour of donkey 15, 17 :

foal 118; white markings 18
Colt 11, 74 : buying 24
Columbine 108-109
Command words 58
Condition and turnout class 74
Condition — poor 90, 93, 100, 106, 108
Conformation 9, 15, 18, 19-22 : D.B.S. rules 19
Confused condition 110
Constipation. 106 : foals 140
Cookie **28**
Cordelia **91**
Coronet **19**, 87, 89, 104
Cost of keeping donkeys 25
Cotton wool 111
Coughing 90, 99
Covering (stocking) 120, 121
Cow hocks 22
Cracks in hooves 89
Cross 15, **16**, 18, **19**
Crupper 66, 67, 72

Damascus ass 15
Dandy brush 51
Dandylion Handsome **16**
Daphne 33
Day shelter *see* Shelter
Dead foal 149-150
Deadly Nightshade 33
Death 104, 109, 149, 154
Defecate *see* Dung
Dehydration 106
Desdemona **91**
Diarrhoea *see* Scouring
Dicaracide 90
Dichlorvos 93
Dictyocaulus 90
Disinfectant 37, 111
Dismounting from a donkey 69
Distressed donkey 110
Docks 33
Donkey as herd animal 57
Donkey Breed Society (D.B.S.) 8, 9, 13, 23, 26, 50, 70, 73, 74, 86, 115 : area representative 23, **135**,

154; driving section 70, 73; points of a donkey 19; registered studs 24, 120; rules of conformation 19; stud book 13, 24, 83, 115, 118, 119
Donkey class at show 78
Donkey rug 99, 110, 153
Donkey Sanctuary 15, 25, 35, 154
Drenching 92, 102
Dressage 70
Driving 13, 70-73, **71**, 84, 126
Driving class 74
Driving pad **65**, 66, 71
Driving section of D.B.S. 70, 73
Dung 32, 106, 128 : foal 140; foal eating dung 140
Dunkels, Miss Marjorie **75**

Ears 10, **19** 54, 95 : conformation 20; foal's ears **135**, 135
Eating problems 82
Egyptian Ass 15
Elderly donkey 106, 150-53 buying 11; exercise 56; training 63; teeth **82**, 82, 152
Electric fences 35
Elizabeth Ann **91**
Enteritis 141
Entire donkey 11; buying 12
Equine influenza 26, 100
Equine insurance 50
Esmeranda **16**
Ether 102
Euphorbia 33
Ewe neck 21
Eyes **19**, 54, 95-8, conformation **20**, 21; ointment 96; running **98**, 99, 107
Exercise 31, 54-6, **55**, 89, 104, 126; elderly donkey 152
Exercise cart 72
External boundary fence 35

Face conformation 20 : swelling 107
Faeces *see* Dung
Farrier 23, 26, 62, 84-9, 126
Fat donkey *see* Overweight
Fatten, to 30
Fear 106
Feeding bowls 45, 102
Feeding *see* Food
Feeding in-foal mare 124-5 : rejected foal 147-9; times 44
Feet **19**, 39, 84-9, 104, 126 : cleaning 53, 77, **84**, 87; conformation 22; foal's feet 145; lifting 10, 62; protective gristle at birth 130; trimming 26, 84 *see also* Hoof
Felt saddle 67 : for panniers 66
Fencing 31, 32, **34**, 35
Fetlock **19**, 36
Field *see* Land and paddock
Filing teeth 84
Filly 11
Finding a home for donkey 154
First milk *see* Colostrum
First teeth 81
Fleur **151**
Flies 37, 39, 45, 93, 95-8, **96** : elderly donkey 152
Floor for stable or shelter 39
Fly repellant *see* Insect repellant
Fly veil **97** : elderly donkey 152
Foal : buying 11; cost 113; death 134, 149; encouraging to suckle 138; feeding 138, 142, 144; first outing 140; gestation period 113, 124; growing foal 139-45; hand rearing a foal 146-9; inherited characteristics **117**, 117, 118-20; navel 125; newborn foal 134-9; leading 140; picking up **141**; preparation 123; pros

and cons of having a foal 112-14; scouring 106; selling 113; sex 124; suckling 134-9; 142, 144; supervision 113, 127, 130-34; two foals 117 see also Birth of a foal
Foaling box 123
Foaling see Birth of a foal
Foetal faeces 140
Foetus 124
Food 42-5, 107 : amount 44; elderly donkey 152; laminitis 89; mixture 44; unsuitable 102; see also Cereal, feeding, grass, hay, ponynuts
Foster mother 147
Foxglove 33
Free return service 121
Frog (in hoof) 86, 89
Frost 102

Gangrene 104
Gelding 11, 12, 24 : as pet 12; buying 12, 24
General troubles 107-11
Genes 124
Gestation period 113, 124
Gilmour, Maureen 114
Girth strap 67, 72
Glands 101
Glucose 147
Grass 33, 42, 78 : spring 42, 44, 89, 102; wet 42, 106 see also Pasture, and Paddock
Grass tummy 42, 126
Grey donkeys 17
Gristle on foal's feet 130
Grooming 29-30, 51-4, 93, 106 : foal 145; elderly donkey 153; newly foaled mare 141; for showing 76-8
Grove Hill Donkey Stud 115
Growing foal 139-45 see also Foal and Weaning
Gymkhana classes 70

Hadrian 76
Hair 95, 104 : falling out 94, 107, 108, 109; matted 108
Half door 38, 38
Half-moon bit 49
Halland Horse Show 75, 76
Haloxon 93
Halter 27, 36, 46, 78 : knotted 36, 47, 76, 77; putting on 46
Hand rearing a foal 146-9
Hands (measurement) 13
Handsome 16
Handy donkey class see Versatile donkey class
Hard food see Cereal
Harness (driving) 70-73
Hawthorn 35
Hay 25, 30, 33, 40, 42-4, 78, 91, 140, 144 : buying 42; mouldy 44, 102, 107; storing 42
Haynet 40, 43, 78 : filler 43
Hazards in paddock 103 see also Poisonous plants
Head 19 : conformation 20, 21
Headband 47, 48, 49
Headcollar 27, 28, 47-8, 76, 77, 78
Heathfield Show 61, : riding class 68
Heating lamp 123
Heaton, Virginia 65, 71
Heels 19, 105
Hen food 102
Herbs 33
Hereditary defects and diseases 118
Hind legs 19 : conformation 22
Hindquarters 19 : conformation 21
Hippomane 124, 132, 133
Hogweed 34
Holly 35
Hoof 19, 52, 54, 84-9, 88, 104 see also Feet
Hoof oil 51, 54, 77, 78
Hoof-pick 51, 86

Horsebox 77 : loading 63, 75 see also Trailer
Horse markets 24
Huggy 16
Hyperlipaemia 30

In-foal mare 124-6
Infection 100, 106, 108, 120 : foal 132, 134, 136, 142
Influenza 100 see also Anti-flu injections
Inherited characteristics 117, 118-20
Insect repellant 96, 109, 110, 111
Insurance 26, 50
Intestinal worms see Worms
Intestines 101, 103, 104, 106

Jack 11
Jenny 11
Jointed bit 49
Jolly 112
Jones, Mrs Ann 68
Joseph 91
Judge 75, 74, 78-80
Jumping 70
Justavius 59, 141
Justinia 137

Katherina of Harbolets 68
Kathleen 52, 63, 138
Kelly 28
Kicking 10, 60, 64, 90
Kingsley-Lewis, Cleone 70
Knibb, Austen 135
Knotted halter see Halter

Laburnum 33
Lameness 104, : feet 86-7, 88-9
Laminitis 88-9
Lamps (driving) 73
Land 31-7 : see also Grass, Paddock and Pasture
Leading 27, 61
Leading rein 48, 76
Legs 19, 104 : conformation 13, 22

Lice 94, 126 : elderly donkeys 153
Licking foals dry 135, **136**
Lifespan 12, 57
Lifting feet 10, 24, 52, 58, 62
Ligaments at base of tail 128, 129
Lips swelling 107
Liquid Paraffin 106
Listlessness 99, 101, 110 : foal 138, 139, 142, 143
Lockjaw 109, 110
Long-reining 58, 72
Louse powder 94
Lumps and bumps 108, 111
Lunging 56
Lungs 90, 101 see also Lungworm
Lungworm 25, 92-3, 99; elderly donkeys 153
Lying down **28**

Maidenhead 23, 26
Maize (flaked) 44
Mallow 34
Mane **19, 52, 53,** 72, 109
Mange 94-5
Mare 11, 12-13, 113, **117** : buying 24, 116; feeding 44 see also Section on breeding 112-46
Mare is about to foal 127-9
Marius **55, 91**
Mastitis **103,** 103-4, 142
Mating see Covering
Mayfield (Sussex) Nativity **64**
Meal times 29
Measurements of donkeys 13
Meat 35
Meconium 140
Medicine : colic 102; 'cupboard' 111; to administer 102, 111
Membranes 129, 130
Menier **6, 55**
Mice 45
Milk analysis 147 : cow's milk 147; substituted milk

142; teats dripping milk 128
Milk dung 140
Milk teeth 81
Milking a donkey mare 138-9, 146
Mineral supplements 45
Moira 24, 26, **53, 125, 136,** 139
Monkshood 33
Mouldy hay and straw 44, 102, 107
Mounting a donkey (riding) 68
Mucus 94, 99, 100
Mud 104, **105**
Mud fever 104-5, **105**
Mules 118

National Equestrian Centre 74
Near side 27, 68
Neck **19** : conformation **20,** 21
Neck collar (driving) 71
Negasunt 110
Nellie **16, 19**
Netting 35
Nettles 33 : stings 108
Nervous donkey 29
Nose and throat 99-101
Nose, running 99-101, 107
Night shelter see Shelter
Nightshades 33
Nilverm 92
Nipping 60
Nits 94
Nitrogen 42, 89
Noseband 46, 47, 48
Nostrils **19,** 54, 100 : swelling 107
Novice class 74
Numbers (at show) 78

Oats (crushed) 44
Oat straw 39
Oberon **71**
Obese donkey see Overweight donkey
Obstacle race see Versatile donkey class

Oestrus 12, 120, 121, **122,** 143, 146
Ophthalmic antibiotic 96, 98
Orchids 34
Origin of donkeys 7
Ostermilk 147
Overeating 102
Overfeeding 89
Overshot jaw 83
Overweight donkey 30, 45, 89, 152

Paddock 29, 37, 91, 103, 120, 123 see also Grass, Land and Pasture
Pain 99, 101-3, 104, 110, 129, 145
Pairs (driving) 72
Panniers 56, **65**
Parascaris equorum 90
Parasites 32, 89-95, see also Worms
Parrish, Kim **76**
Parrot mouth 83
Parting 153-4
Pasture 90-92 see also Grass Land and Paddock
Peat 39
People with Long Ears 23, 27
Piebald 15
Pig food 102
Pig wire 35
Pin-toed 22
Placenta 129, 131
Plaiting 22
Playing 54, **55,** 117
Plurenden, The Lady 18
Pneumonia 100, 101 : foal 141, 143
Points of the donkey **19,** 19-22
Poison 102, 106 : meat 35; plants 33, 44, 56, 102, 120
Ponynuts 29 : amount to feed 44
Post-and-rail fencing 34
Potatoe plants 33
Prefix 115
Pregnancy testing 124

Preparing for a foal 123-4
Presence 22
Primrose 34
Privet 35
Progeny of the stallion 119
Prolapse 106
Punishment 60
Putting to sleep 154

Queen Anne's Lace 33

Ragwort 33, 44
Rashes on skin 108
Rasping teeth 84
Rats 45
Red worms 89
Registered donkey 13, 115
Registered stud 24, 120
Reins 66, 67
Rejected foal 146-9 : feeding
    147-9; weaning 149
'Rescuing' a donkey 15
Riding 13, 30, 66-70, 74, 84,
    126 : aids 67; maximum
    weight 66; minimum age
    67; training donkey 67
Riding class 68, 74
Ringworm 108
Roan 17
Rolling 101-2, 116, 133
Rubbing 94
Ruffs Orchard Donkey Stud
    23-4, 26, 115
Rug see Donkey rug
Running nose 99-101
Rutilus 16

Saddle, felt 66, 67
Saddle soap 50
Sally 16, 150, 151
Salt 111, 126, 144
Salt lick 40, 144
Salt water 99, 111
Sarah Jane 91
Sawdust 39
Scabs and sores 94, 95, 104,
    105, 108 see also Hair
    falling out and skin with
    bare patches
Scissors 77, 111

Scouring 90, 106 : foals and
    youngstock 106, 142
Scratches 110, 111
Season see Oestrus
Seedy toe 88, 87-8
Settling in your donkey
    26-31 : first day 29
Shafts (driving) 71, 72
Shampoo 76, 77, 94
Shed see Shelter and Stable
Sheep and cattle 90
Sheep netting 35
Shelter 31, 37-40, 38, 95, 96,
    106, 107 : bedding 39;
    door 38-9; floor 39; for
    foal 113, 123; at stud 120
Shivering (foal) 135
Shock 102
Shoes for donkey 84
Shouting 12
Show donkey 54 : buying 18
Showing 73-81, 126
Shutting donkey in at night
    29, 39, 87, 109, 120, 123,
    127
Skewbald 15
Skin with bare patches 94,
    108, see also Hair falling
    out and Sores
Simon 91, 114
Sinusitis 100
Size: of donkey 13-15, 14 :
    of foal 118, 125; of
    shelter 37
Snaffle 49, 67
Sneezing 100
Snow 19
Solanacea 33
Sole of foot 86, 88
Sore throat 100
Sores and scabs 94, 95, 104,
    105, 108 see also Hair
    falling out and Skin with
    bare patches
Spasms of the muscles 101
Spots on skin 107, 109 see
    also Sores
Sprain 104
Spurge 33
Stable 28, 29, 37-8, 38, 101,

123 : bedding 39; floor
    39; for elderly donkey
    152; for ill donkey 111;
    stable
    manners 58 see also
    Shelter
Stale see Urinate
Stallion 11, 118-20, 118,
    119, : as pet 12;
    characteristics 118-20;
    class at show 74;
    conformation 118, 118-9;
    progeny 119; temperament
    118-20, 119
Standing 58, 59, 60, 79
Standing out 75, 76
Stick 61
Stings 98, 108
Stirrups and stirrup leathers
    67
Stockholm tar 88
Stocking see Covering
Stomach 101-3
Stoneleigh 74
Storing hard food 45 : hay
    and straw 42
Strain 104
Straining at birth 130
Strangles 100
Strap for neck 36, 66, 97
Straw 26, 39, 123 : buying
    42; feeding 30, 42, 102,
    126
Strip grazing 35
Stroke 99
Strongles 90
Stud 120-22 : buying from
    24; fees 121; fencing 120;
    registered 23
Stud Book see Donkey
    Breed Society Stud Book
Suckling a foal 103
Sugar beet 44, 102
Summerhays, Reginald 147
Supervision 31, 32, 35-7 :
    foal 113, 127, 130-34;
    in-foal mare 128-9;
    foaling 129-31
Sway back 21
Sweet chestnuts 100

Sweet itch 109
Swellings 108 see also
  Bumps and Lumps
Swollen glands 101

Tack 46-50, 74
Tail 19, 107, 109;
  conformation 21, 21
Tandem (driving) 72
Tarquinia 135
Tear duct 98, 99
Teats 103, 104, 125, 127
Teena 69, 128, 143
Teeth 45, 81-4, 82, 83 :
  conformation 21; elderly
  donkey 82, 152; filing or
  rasping 84, 152; foal's
  teeth 142
Temperament 9, 10, 119,
  119
Temperature 100, 111, 135
Terramycin 88
Tetanus 109, 110 : elderly
  donkeys, 152; in-foal
  mares and foals 126 see
  also Anti-tetanus
  injections
Tethering 35-7, 36
Thiabendazole 92
Thin donkey 30 see also
  Feeding
Third-party liability
  insurance 26, 50
Thistles 33, 42
Three-year-old 11
Throat 99-101
Throat lash 48, 49
Timid donkey 29
Tit-bits 27, 29, 30, 45, 60 :
  elderly donkeys 152
Tobacco plants 33
Tomato plants 33
Toxic see Poisonous
Traces (harness) 72
Traffic 30, 63
Trailer (loading) 63, 75 see
  also Horsebox
Training 30, 57-64, 74, 140 :
  for driving 72; for riding

67
Travelling 27, 63, 77, 121
Trimming hooves see Feet
  and Hooves
Trotting 58, 60, 75, 78, 79
Troubles from ear to tail 95-
  107
Tugs (harness) 71, 72
Twisted gut 104
Two donkeys 25, 28, 117
Two-year-old 11 : buying 11
Tying up 58, 62 see also
  Tethering

Udder 103, 104, 124, 127,
  128, 137, 142, 146, 149
Umbilical cord 124, 131,
  130-32 : refusing to break
  132; spraying stump 132
Unchewed food 83 see also
  Teeth
Undershot jaw 83, 83
Upper thigh 19 :
  conformation 22
Urinate 32 : foal 140
Uterus 133

Vacuum cleaner 77
Vacuum grooming kit 77
Vagina 106, 130
Vehicle (driving) 70, 71, 72,
  73
Ventilation 38, 99, 101, 110,
  123, 153
Versatile donkey class 58,
  61, 74, 80
Vetch 34
Veterinary examinations 15,
  23, 25, 30
Veterinary surgeon 23 :
  when to call 83, 87, 89,
  94-6, 98-102, 104, 106-111,
  116, 149 : foal and foaling
  133, 134, 139, 140, 142,
  143, 147, 153
Vipsania 32
Vitamins and minerals 44,
  45, 108, 126 : elderly
  donkeys 152

Vulva 129, 132, 141

Walking 58, 60, 78, 79
Walks 56, 58, 126, 152
Wall of hoof 86, 87, 88
Warble fly and eggs 93
Warts 105
Water (drinking) 31, 37, 40,
  76, 78, 123, 139, 140, 144,
  149, 150
Water, breaking at birth 129
Wax in ears 54, 95
Waxing (teats) 127
Weaning 11, 103, 121, 144,
  145-6 : hand-reared foal
  149
Wheat 102
Wheat straw 39
Wheezing 101 see also
  Breathing
Whip (driving) 73
White donkeys 15, 16, 17
White line (hoof) 86, 87, 88
White markings on
  donkeys 18
White worms 90
Wild donkeys 57, 145
Wire brush 51
Withers 13, 19
Wood shavings 39
Words of command 58
Working donkey 31, 44, 54
Worms and worming 25, 30
  32, 40, 89-92, 102, 106,
  109, 126 : elderly donkey
  153; worm count 93;
  worming foal and young-
  stock 90, 145; new foaled
  mare 145
Wounds 98, 110, 111

Yearling 11
Yew 33
Young donkey 11, 95, 106 :
  buying 11; feeding 44;
  scouring 106

Zebra markings 18
Zinc and castor oil 95, 106,
  107